What others are saying about

"A wonderful book that will fill the heart of any sincere and true seeker, and point the way to the hidden spiritual worlds."

- Damien G., France

"I have never read anything like it in any spiritual teachings, but at the same time very deep inside it feels like I have always known it. It's the way home, the door to most Sacred of all."

- Vladimir E., Netherlands

"Spiritual truth that is Soul stirring! The most direct path back to God explained so I can comprehend it! I will read again and again..."

- Daniel Walton, Washougal, Washington

"Absolutely AMAZING book.. Such inspiration and wisdom all packed into one book. Get ready, get set to catch a wave on the Audible Life Stream back to God."

- Jovana Smith, California

"This book is helping me to avoid all the pitfalls that make life miserable. What it can do for me it can do for you. It reveals the pathway to total mastery in your life."

- John W. Herbert, Parrish, Florida

DIALOGUES WITH THE
MASTERS
THE WAY BACK TO GOD VIA SOUL FLIGHT!

BOOK ONE

BY ALLEN FELDMAN

First Edition

 Direct Path Publishing, Roseville, California

Dialogues With The Masters:
The Way Back to God via Soul Flight, Book One
Copyright © 2014-2015 by Allen Feldman and Heather Giamboi.
All Rights Reserved.
Published in the United States by:
Direct Path Publishing
1911 Douglas Blvd. #85-165
Roseville, CA 95661
www.DirectPathPublishing.com

ISBN-10: 0-9969073-2-7
ISBN-13: 978-0-9969073-2-3

Dialogues With The Masters, The Way Back to God via Soul Flight. 1. Out-of-Body
Experiences 2. Self Realization and God Realization 3. Astral Projection
4. Meditation and Spirituality 5. Heaven

Cover Art painting of Rebazar Tarzs by Heather Giamboi

DEDICATION

This book is dedicated to the Ancient VARDAN Masters. In particular Sri Rebazar Tarzs, Sri Yaubl Sacabi and Sra Kata Daki. They serve the HURAY (God) with all their hearts and work tirelessly to bring VARDANKAR to this bleak world so that Souls may return back to God in a single lifetime and not have to wait millions of incarnations. They are my inspiration.

I also want to thank my wonderful and loving wife who is also a very powerful VARDAN Master in her own right, Sra Gah-Shy-Zah. And last but not least I must thank Sri Paul Twitchell known as Paddar Zask who has opened the door once again to the most direct path back to God.

DIALOGUES WITH THE MASTERS

CONTENTS

INTRODUCTION

There is a group of beings here on Earth of such a high spiritual nature that it staggers the imagination of man. Man, for the most part, does not understand God nor who, or what God is or is not. God cannot really be spoken of, nor defined nor put into a box. IT must be experienced. IT dwells far above the worlds of time and space in what is known by the Ancient Spiritual Travelers of VARDANKAR as the Ocean of Love and Mercy, where it speaks to Soul our true eternal self through the conscious contact with the Audible Life Stream.

I am not speaking in metaphors here nor in symbolism, but in the act of seeing the very face of God and reaching God Realization or TOTAL Awareness. This should be our only goal. To learn to die daily and work with the true Spiritual Travelers until we reach the Atma Lok or Soul Plane and eventually reach God Realization, where we quite literally experience Total Awareness and see the face of God. This does not mean we know all things, for there is always a plus factor and another step to take, and no one Soul can totally know God. But we can have God Realization in this lifetime and become a true Spiritual Traveler ourselves, in order to serve the divine plan and perhaps help free other Souls from the terrible bondage of reincarnation and karma and these lower worlds of matter, energy, time and space.

The ancient VARDAN Masters are far above so called religious gurus, priests and metaphysicians. They are above the angels, saints and other so called guiding lights of truth, for they and they alone speak from the high God Worlds above the Soul Plane and yet dwell in the lower worlds in body.

They are complete men and women who have reached a degree of spiritual perfection, where they can consciously dwell here on Earth and simultaneously in the high heavens, including the Anami Lok and even within the secret dwelling place of the HURAY or God itself known as the Ocean Of Love and Mercy.

God is not a man-like figure nor appears human in any way, shape or form. If one speaks of God as a man or having a man-like appearance, he is mistaken. Yes it is true there are the various Spiritual Rulers of the lower worlds of M.E.S.T. (matter, energy, space, and time) but these are not the one true God the HURAY but only lower manifestations that are a mixture of Spirit, Matter and Mind.

In the pure God Worlds there is no mind, no matter, nor time nor space and Soul, our true God-Self dwells in eternal bliss as a conscious co-worker with God. It is here that Soul takes on its rightful place in the scheme of things, and learns that eternity begins and ends with selfless love for the HURAY and the conscious giving of oneself without ever thinking of reward.

The Spiritual Travelers are here to show man the way back home to the one true God, not in some future lifetime but here and now. They teach man to die daily during his Spiritual Exercises, leave the physical body and boldly venture far above the Physical, Astral, Causal, Mental and Etheric Planes into those high regions, known as the Pure Positive God Worlds where Soul learns through direct perception, and knows all things and exists in a state of SEEING, KNOWING and BEING. In this high state of awareness, Soul possesses a 360 degree viewpoint and is free to travel and has access to the sum total of all Love, Wisdom, Power, Freedom, and beyond.

Man balks at this, claiming it is impossible and tries to grovel at the feet of his space God, a sort of Santa Claus that he begs to offer him favors of a materialistic, emotional and mental nature.

But the true God or HURAY does not care about man's lower embodiments; only about Soul, our true eternal God self, returning to IT and taking Soul's rightful place as a conscious co-worker throughout eternity. This is the purpose of the true Spiritual Travelers and I have had many dealings with them over the years to the point where it was possible to speak with them and write this book.

While it is true that I too am a Spiritual Traveler, I do not claim to have the Love, Wisdom and Power of those Ancient Masters. This may sound strange being I am the Margatma, the Living VARDAN Master, and yet I do not claim to know all things.

I am simply a humble channel for the HURAY whose purpose is to guide those ready Souls back home to God; this and no more.

Some will wonder: if I am a VARDAN Master, why do I know so much less than the Ancient VARDAN Masters?

First, one must remember that whenever one takes up a new physical body, there is a cloak of forgetfulness and the new brain and other bodies may dim the light of Soul in this world.

What I am saying here is that if we judge others and ourselves through the eyes of the mind and materiality, we shall fail on the road back to God. We must have the eyes to see truth and the ears to hear it.

I say unto you that there is always a plus factor and God will use any and all beings who are willing and able to serve IT, no matter what their apparent outer condition is in life.

This is perhaps the entire point. That man has been subjugated to so many external forces that he has lost his true power. This power is of the VARDAN or Holy Spirit; but is not of a psychic nature but of a pure spiritual one. We do not use spirit but spirit uses us! And in the end, we discover that we and Spirit are identical in substance. We are the personalization of Spirit.

As the great VARDAN Master, Sri Paul Twitchell has said: "The least in heaven are the greatest." And this statement is true!

It is not our skills, nor mental nor emotional abilities that count, so much as our willingness to surrender to the VARDAN or Spirit and begin at once on the path of self-discovery through the Ancient Science of Out of Body Tuza Travel.

Therefore I say unto you that no one is perfected in the lower bodies, but as Spirit our true Self Soul, we may find our lower bodies such as the physical, astral or emotional and mental become servants of our true Self Soul, and that Soul and God are cut of the same cloth. We are conscious drops in the Ocean of Love and Mercy. All else, but the HURAY, is an illusion.

In closing this rather long introduction, I wish to thank the great VARDAN Master, Rebazar Tarzs, who has done so much to help me spiritually as he has for countless others. Yaubl

Sacabi, who I cannot say enough good things about and has perfected himself to such a high degree, that he has had to often remind me he is only a humble servant of the HURAY.

In these discourses, you will find the timeless wisdom that brings one the experience of Self and God Realization through the movement of Soul into the various levels or planes of heaven. This path of Out of Body Travel is for the bold, adventurous, cunning and courageous who love truth more than the air they breathe.

Most do not want truth and when it is offered, will run as fast as they can from truth. What they seek is the amusements of this world: human love, sex, power, wealth, health, social approval and the things of this world. They confuse karma with love and are not true spiritual seekers. To them, this book will probably mean little or nothing. But to the bold and adventurous and those who love God more than their attachments and fears this will change them.

If you read this book with an open mind, you too will be changed and will never see life the same.

Allen Feldman, August 2014

1

THE GREAT ANCIENT MASTERS

There is a sickness on this Earth world. This sickness is not about the dichotomy of good versus evil but rather the sleep-like state of not truly recognizing who we are spiritually and what exactly God really is.

To know one's self and to know God has been talked about and philosophized since man first developed language millions of years ago. What I am speaking of here is not a superficial understanding, or mental or philosophical images that strike the imagination, emotions or mind of man ... but something else entirely. The personal experience of one's True God self which occurs during Self Realization and the personal experience of God ITSELF, which occurs during God Realization.

Many will speak of these two topics as if they themselves have had the experience of God ... but upon further examination, and the reading of countless books and the listening to lectures of countless gurus, teachers, masters, religionists, philosophers and so forth; I have come to the conclusion that none of them know anything about the personal experience of God and few have any experience of their True Self, as Soul or that spark or drop of consciousness known in VARDANKAR, the Ancient Science of Total Awareness, as the Ocean of Love and Mercy where dwells the HURAY, the one and only true God above all time, matter, energy and space.

However, there is hope for there is one group of Ancient Masters who do, in fact, lead Souls by the millions back to the personal experience of God Realization.

These Masters have existed on all planets during all times in the history of the lower worlds of M.E.S.T. (Matter, Energy, Space and Time).

The truth is, humanity has always been sick. The illness it has; has little or nothing to do with evil or the harming of others, but with the lack of a certain realization of God that lacks in almost everyone in these lower worlds of M.E.S.T.

The cure for this illness can only be partaken of one Soul at a time, and it has nothing to do with social reform, nor being a "Good" person, or is of a social or moral nature in any way.

Instead, it is the movement out of one's body into these dimensions, planes or worlds into the very heart of God ITSELF.

This is indeed possible, however there are numerous lower rulers or lesser Gods who pose as the one true HURAY or God.

These lower rulers are themselves involved with M.E.S.T. although they have so much power and divine intelligence that almost all are fooled into believing they have reached the ultimate Godhead.

There are as many states of consciousness as there are people in this world, therefore the Great HURAY allows man to choose his God or Gods whether they be social, material, mental or emotional in nature. But ultimately, man must decide whether he desires God or whether he desires to lull in the material worlds.

These material worlds are filled with traps and only the Spiritual Travelers, the VARDAN Masters, understand how a Soul can find spiritual freedom!

This disease that inflicts us is that of the lifetime upon lifetimes and embodiment upon embodiment; but it is mostly due to our lack of personal experience and Divine Wisdom.

This personal experience and Divine Wisdom cannot really come from books, nor lectures, ideas, ideals, emotions or thoughts. It cannot come from any conventional sources of man.

The Spiritual Travelers are way showers. They show one how to leave their physical bodies and venture out boldly into the very heart of God. When Soul transcends the lower worlds of time and space, it gains ISNESS, BEINGNESS, SEEINGNESS and AMNESS. IT, being identical in substance to Divine Spirit and ultimately a particle or drop from the Ocean of Love and Mercy where dwells the Mighty HURAY, knows all things and cries out, "I AM THAT I AM!" Soul knows through direct perception and has no need for a mind at these high levels.

However, a mind is necessary as a tool much like a diving pressure suit is used by a deep sea diver. The mind makes a wonderful servant but a very poor master.

Go with me on the adventure of a lifetime. Your own personal experience of God!

You will find the words uttered by these high Spiritual Travelers are unlike any before read. They are here to guide the bold, the adventurous, the willing and those who love God more than their petty defilements.

They are for the true God seeker!

And so it was I begin my story with some of my meetings with the Ancient VARDAN Masters.

Having spent more time in the various lower worlds than you would believe possible, I found after much practice that I could, through direct projection, be in the presence of certain Masters such as the Great Rebazar Tarzs, who is a Tibetan Lama reported to be well over 500 years old. You would never know it by looking at him for his body is strong and his hair black along with his dark brown penetrating eyes which appear to look right through you and see all. He appears to be in his early 30's.

Now he lives in the Himalayan Mountains of Northern Tibet in a mud hut, and his skin is swarthy and a bit weather worn from the sun and wind.

He stands just under six feet tall, perhaps 180 lbs. and has a closely cropped dark black beard.

He is commonly seen wearing a dark maroon robe with sandals and often carries a gnarled walking stick that is rather useful to lean upon on those mountain trails.

He spends much time in contemplation helping Souls find truth through VARDANKAR, the Ancient Science of Tuza (Soul) Travel. The teaching has had many names; including at one time, it was known as Eckankar from 1965 to 1971 under the great VARDAN Master, Sri Paul Twitchell.

But Eckankar was lost as the high path when there was no one to take over for Paul, and so Rebazar had to take the Rod of Power; and the man who runs Eckankar now is not a true master, as Eckankar has turned into an offshoot path.

Rebazar began to speak.

RT: "You are wondering about Eckankar! And what happened?"

AF: "Yes, it crosses my mind often. Many of us miss Paulji, he was a great Master."

RT: "All VARDAN Masters are great if they serve the HURAY with total selflessness. The trouble is one has to have been to the Anami and one has to be at the very least a 12th initiate, otherwise it is not possible to carry the load."

AF: "I have felt lately that I stumble and feel so inadequate to carry on the great cosmic work."

Rebazar began to laugh and laugh in an almost barking sound that was hearty as the Himalayan Mountain air. He was a powerful man standing almost 6 feet in height and 180 pounds.

AF: "Master, why do you laugh?"

RT: "You know as well as I," he continued laughing. "This world we live in is a hostile place for Soul. Is it not better to serve God badly than to serve the Kal well?"

I nodded in agreement.

AF: "Master, I am beginning to see that I must serve no matter what. Something compels me to do this."

RT: "A great driving force. It is that of selflessness. Come now, there is much work to be done. I do not have all day. Let's get to it."

AF: "I am ready."

RT: "Let us begin with this. All men are fools. It is the nature of man to be a fool. The sooner we understand this, the better! What we desire in these works is not to overcome our foolishness as many falsely believe, but to transcend the limitations of the human state and replace it with the God state. In order to do this, there is only one way; through VARDANKAR, the Ancient Science of Tuza Travel. But the enemies of truth are everywhere.

"They lurk in our own fears, and insecurities and attachments to dogma and religion. They lurk in the very depths of our own psyche! That's right. The enemy of truth is no farther than our own mirror; for if we look into a mirror, we shall see the Kal or negative power peering back at us!" Rebazar laughed again, even harder than before.

Then continued: "Man does not want truth! He desires illusion. He desires his space Gods who he falsely believes will make him happy, but this is not so! Man cannot find truth nor happiness in the lower worlds, for in the end, the joy will turn to pain and misery for it is the nature of the Kal or negative power to alternate from light to dark, happiness to sadness, pain to pleasure and back again."

"What fools most is that sometimes these cycles of alternating opposites take years or even centuries to move from one to another. In the case of the Astral lower world heavens, a being or Soul may occupy what appears to them to be a heavenly paradise on the Astral world or second plane, for hundreds even thousands of years. This gives the illusion of permanence and eternity, but it is an illusion. Soon, such a Soul will find itself back on Earth or one of the other countless planets and universes dealing with negativity, decay and death."

"No soul will find happiness, nor rest for long, as long as they refuse to go with the Spiritual Travelers into the very heart of God or HURAY and achieve spiritual liberation."

"When one is not liberated, they are enslaved!"

AF: "What is the purpose of the lower worlds?"

RT: "Yes...they are to temper Souls and help them reach perfection...they are not permanent places, but are destroyed every few million years in order to make anew. They are very dark places where Soul finds it is generally out-created by its own lower bodies, mainly the mind and somewhat lesser the emotions or astral influences. These Kal forces compete with the VARDAN for domination and the Kal generally will win in the short run, but the VARDAN always wins in the long run because that is the way these universes are set up... to educate Souls."

"Now listen. I have spent enough time answering questions and I wish to discuss the topic of the Ancient VARDAN Masters. We are a group who have a sworn duty to see to it that every Soul is given the opportunity to return to the higher worlds and ultimately reach the great HURAY and become a VARDAN Master themselves."

"Yaubl Sacabi is in charge of this, if you could say in charge, for the HURAY ITSELF oversees the operations of Soul's return to IT, via various channels that IT uses."

"These include the Silent Ones who are mighty beings beyond man's imagination. They live, move and have their being within the very heart of the HURAY and issue out ITS instructions. They run the various planes and universes, and their training is beyond man's imagination. In order for a Soul to become a Silent One, IT has generally already made it to VARDAN Mastership and then scarcely one out of 10,000 applicants pass the tests."

"Becoming a VARDAN Master is child's play when compared with meeting the tests of becoming a Silent One."

"They work as a group and when they issue their orders, the VARDAN Masters generally will obey for they know the Silent Ones work directly with the HURAY on a conscious basis for the good of the whole."

"Another group you should be familiar with is the 9 Unknown VARDAN Masters. They are hidden from all but the most sincere and generally will not work with anyone unless needed."

"They work in secret on the universal plan."

"More visible is myself, Yaubl Sacabi, Rami Nuri and Fubbi Quantz. As you know on each and every plane, there is a VARDAN Temple of Golden Wisdom where truth seekers may study one of several volumes of the Shariyat-Ki-HURAY, which is the Holy Book of VARDANKAR."

"Yaubl Sacabi and Fubbi Quantz are in charge of the first two volumes; Fubbi being in charge of the first volume and Yaubl the second. I cannot say enough good things about Yaubl Sacabi as I know you can't either. He is very old. Some say older than time but this is a joke. But he is very old and wise. All VARDAN Masters have a wiseness about them, but the new ones such as yourself must be patient, for the human psyche will rebel against self-surrender and there can be trouble."

"As it was, we had to rush you in your training due to a

certain situation that was occurring in the lower worlds of M.E.S.T. but this as you know, is not about you but about those Souls who desire to return, and have been chosen by the HURAY to return to IT. There must always be a way shower or Living VARDAN Master."

"We have each taken our own turn in doing this but now is your time, not because you are greater than your fellow man, but because it is the will of the HURAY and you have agreed to serve in this respect."

"One of your greatest obstacles is to overcome personality worship and man's desire to place another person, such as a Spiritual Master above them and worship him from afar."

"Man is lazy. He does not want to work. He does not want to think. He fears leaving his body. Man has been doing this for so long that he most naturally desires to worship others, rather than take responsibility and walk side by side with the Living VARDAN Master into the shining worlds of light and sound; eventually into the very heart of God ITSELF!"

"You must do this. You must tell the world or rather the individual that he is great in spirit and that he should not worship any man, but follow the Living VARDAN Master into the very heart of God ITSELF!"

"You are the most humble of humble servants, for you, as the Living VARDAN Master, must be the way shower and help guide Souls past the rocks and shoals of death, into the Pure Positive God Worlds."

"I can tell you this. Your humility will be tested 10 million times. Your patience also; you will find that most do not want truth but they secretly desire the things of this world!"

"Few seek God and fewer still seek truth. Man is like a child, but there are those Souls who desire God more than life ITSELF and will follow your instructions. You must make it clear to man why you are here. Not to be worshiped but to bring spiritual liberation and the personal experience of God Realization to anyone who is willing to work towards this noble goal."

"There is no other reason for you being here than this."

"I can say no more about it than this."

"You need to stop feeling sorry for yourself and start taking your responsibilities more seriously, for you have been chosen to set the record straight once and for all and guide those ready Souls into their own spiritual greatness."

And with that, Rebazar ended the discourse.

There is little that Sri Rebazar Tarzs does not see. When he gazes at you, it's as if he is looking right through you and knows all there is to know about your past, present and perhaps even future. He does not abuse this power for he knows that most become uncomfortable with this. Most men do not know what real truth is. They fancifully suppose that truth is something that it is not, instead of the living breathing truth of the Holy Spirit or voice of God known among the Spiritual Travelers as the VARDAN.

Just as there is nothing you can hide from the VARDAN, there is nothing you can hide from the Master. But the Master will never interfere with your life or invade your personal space unless given permission therefore, it is important if we desire these great beings in our lives to ask them for their help. Most assuredly, they will grant it if we are sincere about finding God. But they are definitely not here to give man pleasure, entertainment nor emotional comfort, nor the things of this world. Although one may or may not find them, it is not their job to give us what we want but rather what the VARDAN desires us to have, whether that is wealth, health, or a high state of consciousness.

2

WHY THE GODS OF MAN ARE ANGRY

RT: "I wish to talk about why the Gods of man are angry. In the beginning, Souls existed beyond time and space but were in an unconscious state almost as if sleeping."

"The undifferentiated atoms or Souls flowed out of the very fabric of God or the HURAY in its humble abode of the Ocean of Love and Mercy, but they were not giving to one another. They were in a state of bliss for sure, but were not conscious and as such, needed a spiritual education so that they might become conscious and take their rightful place eventually as conscious co-workers or co-creators. This has and always will be the purpose of the lower worlds: that is to give Souls an education and have them return to God."

"However, man was deceived by the Kal Niranjan or king of the negative into thinking that the purpose of life was to remain in the regions of time and space and serve his fellow men."

"This, in the end, proved a grave mistake but a necessary one, in order that Souls gain experience here."

"It was a part of the divine plan of the HURAY, as administered through the various lords, rulers and other members of the spiritual hierarchy."

"The Kal and Brahm were to put Souls through every imaginable experience from the lightest to the darkest. The lower worlds consisting of opposites, there would be little or no rest for Souls who chose to remain here. They would experience all manner of things in seemingly never ending incarnations. Both the so called positive qualities such as love but also the negative opposites such as hate. They would wallow in the five passions of the mind and play with one another exchanging, and creating and working out karma in a seemingly endless span of lifetimes in the various lower worlds, including many planets in the Pinda or physical worlds; but also many incarnations upon the various Astral regions, Causal regions and even high regions upon the Mental plane and Etheric.

"Eventually, Souls would begin to get tired of this endless span of lifetimes and clamor for the true Godhead.

"But the Kal always was cunning and has tried its best to keep Souls occupied and fighting one another or trying to turn the Earth world into a golden age utopia."

"It is the job of the Kal to prevent Souls from escaping and it is Soul's job to escape so that it may become a useful Spiritual Traveler ITSELF and a conscious channel for HURAY."

"What does all of this have to do with the topic of why man's Gods are angry with him? It is simply this that I want to point out and little more. That man has played the fool. By his refusal to seek truth and to listen to the Spiritual Travelers, he has agreed by default to remain in this lower world prison, and because he places the lower realities above the higher goals of reaching the Pure Positive God Worlds and partaking of the great Audible Life Stream, he must pay for this in the form of suffering."

"It is not a punishment but an unavoidable fact that when Soul refuses God, IT will suffer at the hands of the lower creations."

"To refuse God is to reject God and to reject God is to

reject that eternal part of ourselves that is alive. When we reject life itself, we fall prey to death and deterioration."

"You should know about this! It cannot be avoided. To place anything above God is to put on a pedestal death. For anything other than God, the true HURAY, is an illusion and is essentially dead in nature. Death leads to death and life leads to life."

"The more conscious Soul is of the will of God, the more this factors in. For when we consciously choose death over life or Kal over the HURAY, it is one thousand times worse than when we are asleep."

"We have now made a decision: To reject God of ITSELF. And we must pay for this in some way. Not because God is angry with us but because we are breaking the universal law of life; that we must evolve and grow spiritually."

"When we choose to delay this spiritual evolution, we choose death or atrophy. When we choose to grow spiritually, we choose life. But seeking certain psychic powers is not the way to God. It is a trap. We must truly seek God and not the lower rulers who offer only illusions, although these illusions are grand illusions much like most men see."

"The Kal is clever as you know and will put up all forms of illusion, replacing one with another; as soon as we see through one, another is placed before us."

"The only way to get around this is to find the perfect Spiritual Traveler and place our attention upon him. Then we are protected from illusion; although we still must deal with it, it no longer dominates our lives, that is, provided we listen to the Spiritual Travelers or VARDAN Masters."

"They know what is best for our spiritual growth but they also know that man must have freedom to choose. This freedom of choice is a two-edged sword. It can make you great or it can be your ruination."

"The truth is God does not really care. God remains unconcerned. As long as Souls have an opportunity to choose IT, the divine plan is in place. The Spiritual Travelers are there to allow man to find the HURAY, but man must set aside his petty differences and opinions, and become humble before the spiritual Travelers. Then he may begin his journey or ascent into the God Worlds."

"But only after he has found sincerity and clarity in his desire to find God within this lifetime; and not fall for the petty trap of waiting until death to find God."

"If man foolishly chooses to wait until the death of his physical body, what assurance does he have that he will find truth upon his death? None I say. This is one of the great traps of religion and philosophy: always offering something in the future that never comes."

"We must take hold of truth now as you well know! Stop wasting time."

"Until we do this, our universe is without order and the more we understand the nature of life and yet, refuse to move towards God, the more difficult life becomes. For when we consciously deny the presence of God in our lives because of fear or dogma, we are moving towards birth and death and more birth and death. This accounts for man's great suffering and also the almost countless incarnations on Earth and other planets and planes."

"That is all for now!"

3

THE GOALS OF VARDANKAR

RT: "I wish to discuss with you this evening about the goals of VARDANKAR. This is not your usual topic for the goals we have on the high path are entirely and utterly different than those goals that most men seek."

"First off, I want to say that man is in utter opposition to this Kal or negative power. He is entirely at odds with it, for it desires to enslave him and control his consciousness. It will try and trap him inside his body if possible. When this is no longer possible due to man's experience in out of body travel, the Kal will try and fool him into thinking that spiritual freedom and happiness lay in one of the many lower Astral regions. Still further, some make it into the higher Astral Plane where there is much light and sound and beauty. No sooner than Soul reaches these regions, the various rulers are there to fool us into thinking we have reached the end of our journey."

"The beautiful book: *The Tiger's Fang* by Paul Twitchell illustrates this point in an amazing way as does many of Paul's books. As pointed out earlier, Paulji was an amazing VARDAN Master for he was humble enough to allow the great cosmic Sound Current or VARDAN, to channel through his writing. You can do the same. But it takes great humility and a child-like devotion to Spirit or the VARDAN."

"You are a new Master so there is much you need to learn. One day, if you are sincere, you will find truth in a way that will completely astound you. You will truly understand you are a God among other Gods and know the mysteries of Divine Love at a deeper level than you know of now. This is true of All Souls."

"All must learn humility no matter what their position is in life. Whether they are the Living VARDAN Master or the most humble of homeless men laying in the gutter, all Souls are great before God. It's just a matter of spiritual realization."

"However, some foolishly take this too far and believe they do not need a teacher, but can find spiritual truth on their own."

"This is not true. Most can't get out of the Astral region let alone find the Atma or 5th plane where dwells the great Sat Nam, ruler of this region who is the first true manifestation of the HURAY."

"Most men are so busy trying to control their environment that it never occurs to them that their consciousness is the key. Or worse, they realize this but fail to see the difference between, say, the astral awareness and that of the Godman who always dwells in the Anami Lok and above or that 10th region 5 planes above the Soul Plane where God Realization begins."

"It is not until the 12th plane that one finds the true Ocean of Love and Mercy but still, as you know, there is more above this region."

"We cannot truly understand God; only experience IT in our own unique way. And yet, each experience brings us truth."

"Books only dull the mind of man unless they are written by a true Spiritual Traveler or one who has touched the hem of God's robe and come back down to attempt to communicate the way back."

"We must learn to die daily. This is not as scary as it sounds, because once we leave the body we are protected, as always, by a Spiritual Traveler who will make sure no harm comes to us. Dying daily means we leave our physical body and venture into the various worlds and Golden Wisdom Temples where we gather the great cosmic current, also known as the Audible Life Stream or VARDAN."

"This VARDAN is what sustains everything and sustains all known and unknown universes upon universes, and issues forth from the Great HURAY as Light and Sound."

"Within its voice is all Love, Wisdom, Power and Freedom, and yet it is more than even this! It is the breath of life itself: the consciousness that sustains all and is all. And yet, it is not the HURAY but the Spirit of the HURAY."

"Continuing on, I cannot overemphasize the importance of participation in this Light and Sound through service and being active."

"The yogis have it all wrong! Man cannot stay in a passive state of meditation and expect to find truth. He must become a part of truth. He must participate in truth!"

"We are the living, breathing truth and if we don't give truth out and participate in the Audible Life Stream, then we die and troubles will develop. I know this has happened with you. But now is the time to give and be a conscious channel for the HURAY."

"The past does not exist except in the present, so rejoice; you have found truth and can now serve God!"

"Those who are spiritually lost must embrace the ISNESS and BEINGNESS of Truth. They must let go of all dogma and follow a true Spiritual Traveler into the very heart of life or God and venture into the Soul Plane through the methods given them by the Spiritual Travelers."

"Most do not want this therefore they suffer. The Living VARDAN Master sees this suffering and has great compassion. You are beginning to become aware of your inner side, that of the VARDAN and becoming more conscious of it. As you know on the outer, you are imperfect and flawed just like any human being. But inwardly, the VARDAN is taking you over."

"This is necessary for we have much work to do together to gather up the ready Souls who desire to reach Self Realization on the Soul plane or Atma Lok and God Realization on the Anami Lok and beyond."

"Over the coming years, if we are successful, there will be many new VARDAN Masters; as many are now coming and have come to this world to serve."

4

THE VARIOUS PLANES OF GOD: PART 1

RT: "We are going quickly so pay attention. There is little time, as the evening is late, and I will have to go soon."

AF: "I am ready."

RT: "I am going to briefly cover the various planes from the physical on up. Let's start with the Astral. The astral is a plane that is very large. It consists of many regions and is far, far, bigger than the physical worlds. These regions or sub-planes range from the lower astral through mid-astral, and finally the high astral regions.

"They move from darkness to light and, as one moves up, it becomes increasingly nicer, and one feels more and more of Divine Spirit in the air and around him."

"Many go to these regions during their dreams. There are almost countless entities and Souls living on the various astral regions. Many religions have created various heavens on these regions where one may see angels, and many of the things created; I am speaking here of the images one reads about in various religious works such as angels flying around playing harps and colossal buildings."

"The astral, being far less dense than the physical and

containing far less matter, forms much more quickly than the physical, meaning thoughts and feelings manifest. For example, in the physical if we want a house, it can take many months to build it or acquire the money to buy it."

"In the astral, we may simply imagine something and it can form much more quickly. This is the plane of emotions. The colors are brighter and the flowers more fragrant than in the physical. The higher we go on the astral, the more beautiful and the deeper the illusion is that we have reached the God worlds."

"But the astral is only the second plane above the physical world. In the astral is a vast city where the Lord of this world resides. His name is Jot Niranjan and he sustains all of the astral and physical worlds with the great power that moves through him as it descends. He is worshiped by countless Souls who beg for his favor. He has chiseled features and generally does not appear as a man, but exists as pure negative energy."

"He has two faces or poles. One pole is of the positive and the other is of the negative. Thus he has love and hate, anger and compassion, greed and generosity, etc."

"It is the nature of his worlds to have opposites as it is the nature of all the lower worlds, from the Etheric down to the physical."

"One may chant the word Kala (pronounced Kaaaa Laaa) and tune into this place. But be careful. Without a Spiritual Traveler, you may get trapped here and believe you have reached the ultimate heaven."

"There is said to be a museum where all known past, present and future inventions exist. Many inventors go to this museum during the dream state."

"The buildings are enormous in certain regions of the Astral plane."

"Most people who engage in so called astral projection are only visiting the lower to mid parts of the astral, and falsely believe they are making great spiritual strides. Nothing could be further from the truth, as you know!"

AF: "Yes Master. It seems that the new age movement is almost entirely based on the astral state of consciousness. Also the E.T.'s, who visit us, follow this type of cosmic consciousness."

RT: "Yes, it's true; most of the E.T.'s are scarcely on the astral plane although some do make it to the causal. Rarely the mental and yet, they are asking humanity to listen to them. I can hardly blame them for man seems to be bent on self-destruction but some of these E.T.'s only desire to enslave mankind. This is little more than politics and religion and has nothing to do with the attainment of spiritual perfection by reaching the Atma Lok and the Anami Lok."

AF: "Yes Master, I agree."

RT: "Of course. Moving on to the next plane, we find the causal. Here past life memories are stored in what is known as the Akashic records. All past lives from the astral and physical are stored here. These records are very detailed but not nearly as detailed as the Soul records which include all of Soul's experiences from the Atma Lok on down."

"I should point out that there are rooms, as you have witnessed some of them, where one can sit in a chair and view their past lives on what appear to be large 3 dimensional TV screens. One can go to any moment, if allowed access to these records, and play them forwards, backwards, and jump around."

"We can search through them at amazing speeds and find whatever we are looking for. The records include all sensations but again, are not nearly as complete as the Soul records which are, from the view point of Soul, our true God self. But I will cover that a bit later."

"The causal plane has an orange color and many who wear orange robes are tuned into this plane."

"I will not cover this in detail right now, but each of the planes has at least one Golden Wisdom Temple where a VARDAN Master teaches the Ancient Science of Out of Body Travel, mostly to students in the dream state."

"I should say that between each plane is an area of darkness known as the void, and there are several of these voids. Often a Soul will touch one of these voids or dark regions and proclaim that God is NOTHING!"

"These regions, as you know, are filled with darkness and energy and appear impenetrable. The poor Soul who wanders into these dark zones is confused or worse, believes he or she has found Self or even God realization and proclaims that he possesses truth."

"There is a certain wisdom and realization that occurs in these dark zones or regions, and a certain amount of the cosmic light and sound that pours forth, therefore it is very easy to think you have reached the top of all the worlds and met God when, in fact, you have done no such thing. This is still another reason why the Spiritual Travelers are necessary in order to protect against this happening, and take the student past these zones into the next plane, and so on."

"The great void is the last zone or region and is the most

difficult to travel past. Without a Spiritual Traveler, it is close to impossible. It is the dark region just before the Soul plane or Atma Lok. But there is a zone similar between each of the planes in order to keep Souls contained inside them, until they are ready to move on. For most men, the Lords of Karma who administer the laws of karma on behalf of the Kal, will see to it that a man goes wherever he has earned in that respective lifetime."

"A man may be brought up by the Lords of Karma from say, the Earth world to a stay on the mid-astral, because this man has earned some good karma. This man may live in a relative state of ease and find things very pleasant. This would give the illusion of being in heaven, and the life spans on this plane could be anywhere from a few hundred years, to millions of years in extreme cases."

"This gives the illusion of eternalness, but it's just a trick made by the Kal to try and fool men into thinking they have found heaven. Then they incarnate back to Earth."

"Some say there is no way to go beyond their respective plane. But these are, generally, those who are not followers of VARDANKAR.

"The true VARDANists know that they can leave their body at will and travel to any of the planes of God; that is, provided they have earned that right through study and initiations from the Master. Many come back and study with the various VARDAN Masters over, and over again, therefore they have earned the right to start at a higher evolution or evolvement than others. This only means they may find it easier to, say, visit the astral plane than others, who lack the memory and experience of previous training.

"When Soul takes on a new body, it forgets most of what it

remembers and this is good in most cases. Imagine, if you will, if a man could remember one million or one billion lifetimes! His puny brain might be overwhelmed and it could be impossible to carry on his daily life for impressions, memories and feelings could overwhelm him from the past; so the HURAY, out of great compassion, draws a curtain of amnesia for most."

"You remember most of your past lives or at least a good portion; do you not?"

AF: "Yes Master. I was mostly a fool. But I did have my moments of realization."

RT: "Yes, this is true. Most men live their lives as fools, for it is the human state of consciousness that is of an animalistic nature. Man does not understand this. He thinks he is a human body or human state of consciousness with a Soul, but it is the other way around! Soul takes on the various bodies, the bodies don't take on a Soul but Soul takes on these bodies. Then the mind begins to out-create Soul."

"This subject is of vast importance to the true God seeker. We cannot hold our previous state of consciousness too closely. We must be willing to let go or be detached from it. Otherwise we cannot leave our body effectively. We must develop detachment to our cherished opinions, beliefs, and so forth."

"Then we can begin to study with the Spiritual Travelers; that is provided that we are worthy and ready."

"Readiness has nothing to do with merit but, actually the HURAY chooses those souls who are ready to return to IT."

"On the surface, there seems to be no rhyme nor reason to who is chosen, but the HURAY has ITS reasons, if you can call them reasons. As you know, you cannot judge the greatness and worthiness of a soul through looks, intelligence, or position in life; nor by job, occupation, interests, nor social standing, nor personality. These are all of the human state of consciousness and temporal in nature."

"Now after crossing this minor void between the causal plane and the mental plane, we enter into the mental plane. The plane of the universal mind power! Few reach this plane, for it is far above the physical, astral and causal regions where most Souls experience life in the lower worlds."

"Many religions have their heavens on this plane. Again, there are many regions on this plane, much like there are countries and cities and places on Earth. Hawaii, for example, is much different from the city of Baghdad. One is a desert; the other a tropical paradise. They both exist on this Earth world."

"The ruler here is known as Sohang. Most so called gurus, and other so called great thinkers and religionists do not even make it this far, but stop somewhere on the astral or causal plane."

"But it must be said that the light here is much brighter and Soul is given the strong impression that it has reached the dwelling place of God. Nothing could be further from the truth. This is only the 4th plane and no more than this! The life spans here can be into the millions of years, therefore it gives the impression that all beings here are eternal in nature. But this is just an illusion made by the ruler of this plane."

"Sohang does not show his face, for he is faceless and is an all pervading consciousness that mesmerizes men and causes them to believe with all their heart that they have made it back to the Godhead. Out of this region all below it is sustained by the great cosmic power and VARDAN that flows from above.

The ruler here has much wisdom and power and acts as a distributor. Being of a much finer and higher vibratory rate than the planes below, Sohang touches into the finer regions of wisdom and knowledge. The beings living here seem to know things through tapping into the great universal mind power."

"But this is the problem. The universal mind power is only a lower world phenomenon. It is a filter that allows Souls to operate in the course vibrations of the lower worlds of M.E.S.T. (Matter, Energy, Space and Time)"

"If one were to travel into the Anami Lok and then view the mental plane, they would see a very course state of consciousness; but looking at it from the human level or astral level, this state appears grand indeed; exquisite by comparison."

"So powerful and filled with Light and Sound is this world of Sohang, that Souls do not want to ever leave and when a Soul manages to briefly visit it from his earth body, he generally becomes some sort of false profit or guru … for all he wants to do is say: I am that I am!! Over and over again. I have met and seen the face of God! I have touched the hem of his robe, I am born anew!"

"This is illusional in nature. These deluded Souls appear enlightened because they are, in a sense. But it is only the light of the mental plane that they carry and not the true Light and Sound that flows from the HURAY ITSELF."

"It is a sort of counterfeit spirituality and if these people were smart, they would join VARDANKAR and follow the Master into the shining worlds above the great void, into the Pure Positive God Worlds of VARDAN."

"This is all for now. We must rest."
"Tomorrow we will cover more."

5

THE VARIOUS PLANES OF GOD: PART 2

I wondered what Rebazar would discuss next. I imagined he was getting ready to speak of the higher worlds, and his mood seemed rather somber as he stroked his beard slightly, as if thinking.

RT: "Are you ready?"

AF: "Yes, Master."

RT: "The reason I seem hesitant is that we are now going to cover the Higher Worlds in this second part of my discourse on this subject ... and man seems to have much trouble."

"He is always comparing things and trying to fit everything into his old state of consciousness. And, frankly, I find this a bit disturbing."

"It is as if man has a one gallon container capable of holding exactly one gallon of water. It will accept no more than one gallon and if you try and put say, two gallons into this container, the water spills out and you always have one gallon no matter what you do."

"Most men are fools and they are eager to compare everything to their own understandings and break it down into

43

what they are used to. So, if you refer to Soul and explain what Soul really is, they will compare what you say with their understanding and then squeeze it into that understanding, even if it does not fit."

"Some will get mad and declare the words of the Master as untrue. These are the ones who do not have the ears to hear or the eyes to see, and they are simply not ready yet."

"Others will, no matter how things are worded or how carefully instructions are laid out, they will break things down and fit them into their present state of consciousness."

"It is sort of like the story of the chicken farmer. There was a chicken farmer, and one day a man began to tell him about eagles and how they can soar far into the air. The man showed the chicken farmer pictures of the eagles, and explained how eagles could swoop down on their prey, and how powerful they were and how great their vision was."

"The chicken farmer seemed very interested in hearing what this man had to say and so the conversation lasted a good hour."

"Then, as if by an act of God, an eagle swooped down from high above and attacked one of the chicken farmer's birds. The farmer managed to throw a few stones at the eagle and scare him off, before he could kill his chicken."

"The eagle soared high into the air deciding to abandon the whole idea of eating that chicken, since it seemed more trouble than it was worth getting rocks thrown at it.

" 'That' … the man said … 'was an eagle.'

" 'No,' the chicken farmer said shaking his head … that was

the meanest chicken I have ever seen in my life.' "

AF: "Yes, it is true ... it seems most are not humble enough to listen to the Master and let go of their old training and understandings to make room for what the Master has to teach them."

RT: "Yes that is, of course, the point but it is even more than this. It is a state of consciousness that we are after. Paul referred to it as Total Awareness. We cannot think our way into heaven, but we must travel there. And this idea is so frightening to most men, that they would rather die than do this!"

"But this is precisely what we teach in VARDANKAR: to die daily. Then we return to our physical bodies born anew. We don't do this to escape, but out of a great love for God and a great desire to return to IT and become a conscious co-worker. We realize that we can have our feet on Earth and our hearts in heaven or, more accurately, our consciousness in the Pure Positive God Worlds, while operating the various lower bodies for the universal benefit and the good of the whole, as conscious co-creators or channels for the HURAY or God."

"Okay. Now I must say the Etheric Plane is the last plane before we reach the Soul Plane, which is the first of the Pure Positive God Worlds of VARDAN. It is here that few escape if they're even lucky to get there. The Etheric is the last region, also known as the top of the Mental Plane, or the area of intuition or high mind."

"When I speak of mind, I am not referring to the human brain, of course, but to that universal mind power that is composed of the positive, negative and neutral forces."

"Man can learn to tap into this universal mind power and when he is fully realized in it, he achieves a form of cosmic consciousness that is very powerful. He is able to raise the dead, multiply food and do all manner of so called miracles. He gains control over the elements. Often this even occurs below the etheric regions."

"But again, the VARDAN Masters are not concerned with this lower world region because it's still a form of bondage or prison for Soul, albeit a much finer prison."

"The life span here is almost unbelievable, numbering from tens of thousands to millions of years, in some cases."

"The irony is that the beings here sometimes end up incarnating back on Earth after very long stays here."

"But few make it this far, so why stay here when we can shed the mental body and operate as pure Soul through direct perception!!"

"After crossing the void, Soul finds itself in the presence of Sat Nam in the Soul Plane or Atma Lok. Here, all things exist beyond time and beyond space. While the etheric and mental planes had a sense of timelessness, it was only because time was so slow."

"The Etheric and Mental Plane can have a sense of depth and wisdom, but it is thinly veiled in illusion."

"Now Soul is stripped of all its lower bodies, and perceives from direct perception and has a 360 degree viewpoint. All negativity and opposites no longer exist, as this is the first pure world of no opposites and the first Pure Positive God World."

"So powerful and filled with light is Sat Nam, the ruler here and first true manifestation of the HURAY, that one hair on his face is the equivalent of 10,000 suns and moons combined."

"When one finds themselves here they often cry out: "I am HE!" "I am that." "I am that I am!"

"Soul now moves and has its being from the epicenter of the great wave emanating through Sat Nam, into this world and all worlds below. He is the great ruler here and distributes the cosmic current, the Audible Life Stream to everything below him."

"The amount of Power, Love, Wisdom and Freedom, emanating from Sat Nam is indescribable."

"This plane, as I stated before, is the first true Pure Positive God World. Having no time, no space, no matter, no energy and Soul being stripped of its lower bodies, we have reached the area of true Self Realization."

Rebazar paused then said in a matter of a fact way, "You are tired. We shall take a break now."

* * * * *

RT: "This discourse is getting a bit long so I shall rap it up. Much of this is covered in other books, such as *The Tiger's Fang* by Paul Twitchell, *The Flute of God*, and some of your books and lectures, as well as more of Paul's."

"Anyway, Soul moves up into the Alakh Lok where Alakh Purusha is the ruler here. Soul, upon entering this plane does not want to leave but, again, we still have not reached perfection in the Ocean of Love and Mercy, only the 6th plane of realization. The seventh is the Alaya Lok and there is a deep humming sound here. The word chanted is HUM."

"I must say, for each plane one may chant the word on that plane. This acts as a sort of homing beacon to tune Soul into the vibrations on that particular plane."

"We simply chant the word of the plane. Like I mentioned, the Alakh Lok the word is HUM as in a deep humming sound with lips pressed together. This is not to be confused with the chant of Aum, which is only of the mental plane."

"As you are well aware, this is one of the great secrets of the Masters or true Spiritual Travelers. Learning to tune into the great Audible Life Stream or Sound Current known as the VARDAN."

"This way of Light and Sound, as mentioned previously takes Soul back to the very heart of God and we may connect with these various planes through the secret teachings of the Spiritual Travelers. One such method involves the chanting of the word for each plane. But there is also the secret word that is given during the VARDAN initiations."

"One can also develop an affinity or love for the Inner Master, who is of the body of the VARDAN or Divine Spirit."

"The Audible Life Stream or VARDAN expresses ITSELF through the personal in the form of the formless Master, who has form. This form joins forces with the conscious Soul who desires to return to God."

"It is really quite simple although I know it sounds complicated at first. The HURAY is so high in vibration and consciousness that those Souls who exist in the lower worlds of time and space cannot touch IT. They must, as I said, travel in

48

awareness to IT. Not through mind, but through spirit or the Audible Life Stream or VARDAN."

"However, the Master or more correctly the Margatma, the Living VARDAN Master, is sent into this world as the way shower to make visible that which lay beyond man's understanding; to act as a sort of bridge."

"If this was not done, it would be virtually impossible for Souls to leave these lower worlds, due to the vast differences in vibratory rates from the lower worlds to the higher."

"Therefore, in a sense, the Margatma, the Living VARDAN Master, is the personalization of the impersonal, a sort of bridge to gather and funnel all of the energies of Soul so that Soul may return."

"Otherwise, the gap or gulf is so vast as to be invisible and unknowable. Too far a jump to make and Souls become trapped."

"Ironically, the Kal will do everything in its power to destroy the Living VARDAN Master and so temporarily destroy this bridge into spiritual liberation."

"By the time a Soul has made it into the Alaya Lok or 7th plane, IT is well established with the Master and can now study through the Golden Wisdom Temples on the various inner planes and through being with the Inner Master at all times."

"The outer works are necessary as a bridge to the inner works, but it must never be forgotten that personal experience with the various God Worlds are the only true realization, and mental and emotional understandings are only shadows of God's true reality and never the goal."

"This is the trouble with religion. It is based on certain feelings and beliefs and text books that are proclaimed as holy works."

"But in the end, we find it is based on the opinions and emotional expressions of men, imperfect beings who know little or nothing about those worlds beyond the lower worlds."

"They are like the fool who thinks that a chicken is an eagle and an eagle is a chicken. They know not the difference between the true God worlds and the dark lower worlds of Kal and, frankly, they do not care. They only desire the things of this world; emotions, thoughts, feelings, opinions and the five passions of the mind; lust, greed, attachment and vanity rule their world. They do not want truth, only a form of self-deluded happiness."

"But the HURAY allows this and lets them choose their own path, knowing full well that they will incarnate in the various lower planes until, once again, they long to return and find the true VARDAN Master who can guide them out of this mess, into the worlds of eternal beingness and truth."

"There is little point in describing further, except to say that the Agam Lok is the plane of the great power: all must understand this power but we will speak of this in a later chapter of this book; I am sure of this. The Anami Lok, where the sound chanted is that of HU (pronounced Hue), is the first plane where true God Realization begins. God Realization moves from the 10th or Anami Lok through the 12th plane, where dwells the HURAY in ITS humble abode in the Ocean of Love and Mercy."

"These are worlds beyond mortal comprehension, as you now know, having been to these worlds many times."

DIALOGUES WITH THE MASTERS

"It generally requires much time to establish oneself in these high, high, worlds in order to filter down the divine Wisdom, Power and Freedom and, of course, Love that flows in an endless wellspring out of the true center of creation."

"We then must be cast down into the lower worlds to serve the great HURAY. But we become like the man who has his head in heaven and his feet on Earth."

"We must carry out the message of VARDANKAR so that other Souls may find the way back just as we have."

"We have learned to die daily and return safely, but more than this we now realize that time and space being an illusion, we never left these worlds. As the saying goes from the true VARDAN Masters: the true VARDAN initiate always dwells in the Pure Positive God Worlds or Higher Worlds."

"Even the most humble of chelas can do this if they will but accept the love of the Master for them as Soul, and know that the Inner Master, that personalization of the VARDAN and HURAY, is always with them and forever guiding them and showing them the way."

"All can find this and all do eventually but, for the most part, man rejects all of this and even attacks it!"

"Man fears truth and wants others to be responsible for him, as a baby desires its mother to take care of him."

"We are not babies, but some Souls are. They are afraid of everything and so they put on their armor suits, and do battle out of fear of truth, and fear of everything."

"They act tough or they act fearful, but all of them are afraid of their divine God self. They are afraid of Truth, for to discover Truth would mean they are responsible for EVERTHING within their own sphere or universe, and they would find they could no longer hide among the sheep or herd instinct that most men cling to out of fear."

"That is all for now. Any questions on this subject matter?"

AF: "No, you have covered a lot. Thank you."

6

OVERCOMING FEAR THROUGH LOVE

RT: "You are wondering how man can overcome fear?"

AF: "Yes Master, it seems fear holds back so many and causes man to cling to his old ways, even when the VARDAN Masters show him a better way."

RT: "Yes, it is of course true, but the real question is why does man cling to these things when he could have a far better life ahead for him, if he would learn the Ancient Science of Out of Body Tuza Travel."

"The truth is kind of shocking. The truth is that man lacks love. He lacks love for himself and he lacks love for his fellow creatures but most of all, he lacks love for God and for truth."

"A man cannot find truth without love and, frankly, most people when pressed will choose convenience over God. They will choose the manifestation of things over God. They will sell their Souls to find happiness and material and emotional success, over God. They only love God, mostly out of a false idea that God will grant them wishes, much like a magical genie."

"This is the worst materialism in man and, frankly not only prevents man from finding truth and finding the HURAY, but also seals his fate in incarnation after incarnation."

"If a man is to find the Master and go back to God, he must love God above all else. Love God, even beyond his own life ... beyond materiality, emotionalism, and the social and economic ties that bind him to this world."

"Religion is the worst! It distorts God and makes God into a sort of Santa Claus who grants wishes of a material, social and emotional nature. It exchanges God for moral codes, it substitutes God for ideas, ideals and personalities. It even tries to substitute God for a dusty old book, as if a book were God?"

"What is the bible but a series of stories. I am not saying there is no wisdom in the bible, but compare the bible with the Shariyat-Ki-HURAY and you will see one book is about emotion and drama, and the other is about Soul finding its way back to God."

"Jesus was a very misunderstood man. He was only a student of a VARDAN Master who went off base and started a religion against the wishes of the Living VARDAN Master of the time."

"And look at what happened? Millions of people were murdered in the name of Jesus! A man who tried to tell the world to love your neighbor as yourself. So what did man do? He killed his neighbor. Tortured his neighbor in the name of Christ!"

"Do you see how the Kal Niranjan plays on the vanity and arrogance of mankind?"

"Religion is an opiate that the masses use in order to hide from truth. You have a book and this book and this master, or dead master or savior, replaces any effort or thinking on the part of the student. They no longer have to think. They no longer have to do anything that requires any effort, other than attending some building once a week and, perhaps, reading a book."

"And all of this is done at the great profit of the leaders who ask for money for giving man little or nothing. Man wants to feel good about himself. He is an emotional creature scarcely above the animal in consciousness."

"The masses will never be ready for VARDANKAR because it is too demanding of their energies. Without love, you have atrophy. You have stagnation."

"The true VARDAN initiate loves God and loves the Master so much, he or she is willing to be a fool rather than hide from God."

"That is all these people are doing, is hiding from God. God demands that man return to IT! Not after death but during life ITSELF! How can we ever be sure what will happen after we die in the body?"

"Is not eternity in the here and now? So when man rejects God in the here and now, has he not rejected God?"

"To delay ones journey to God is foolish but this is what 99.8% of the people of Earth have chosen, and so the VARDAN Masters have to patiently wait, for these are the unready Souls. They will eventually return to God but not anytime soon. They have, in effect, turned their backs on God and yet, claim to be religious and God-like in nature."

"They harp on their good works toward their fellow man, but they fail to see that feeding the body is not the same as nurturing our true Self Soul through partaking of the great cosmic light and sound found in the high, high, God Worlds."

"This and only this: the experience of God will squelch man's thirst for truth!"

7

HOW TO LEAVE ONE'S BODY AND FOLLOW
THE SUPREME PATH BACK
TO THE HURAY

RT: "I will now talk about how to leave one's body and follow the supreme path back to the HURAY."

AF: "Yes Master, I am looking forward to this discourse."

RT: "This, of course, is a very complex topic and I will not be giving step by step directions, for this is the job of the VARDAN discourses, and the various books and lectures on VARDANKAR. It's far too complex to lay out in these few pages and, of course, volumes could be written about the subject."

"However, having said this, there are some basic understandings that go a long way."

"First off, one needs 4 things to return to God."

"They are:
1. The Living VARDAN Master.
2. The Sound Current.
3. The VARDAN initiation.
4. The Spiritual Exercises of VARDANKAR."

"I am, of course, oversimplifying a bit but this list is the essentials and anything on this list is required, if there is any reasonable hope of returning within a person's respective lifetime."

"I would like to pay homage to one of the greatest Souls I have had the pleasure of working with. The great VARDAN Master, Yaubl Sacabi."

All of a sudden, Yaubl appeared before me. I was not shocked in the least for I have seen him many times and am aware of his presence throughout my days and evenings. He is bald headed and has the most amazing brown compassionate eyes that seem to be pools of love. It's as if looking into the Ocean of Love and Mercy. There is a calm quiet Love and Wisdom about this being. His age is beyond human comprehension and yet, one feels the most wondrous sense of inner peace and contentment from just being around him. The room immediately got brighter."

YS: "It is a fact that when a being dwells consciously in the Ocean of Love and Mercy, he or she acts as a channel or conduit for that God force that would ordinarily be too high in vibratory rate to affect man. Yes, there are many descending planes, each lower in vibration but when a being who, exists in body form is consciously dwelling, and has surrendered completely to the HURAY and does all in ITS Name and becomes that which IS; or the ISNESS of the HURAY, then those who gaze into that being's eyes get what is known as the Darshan, or the gaze of the Master."

"The very presence of such a being is as if God or the HURAY ITSELF is making contact with the individual. For this is very much like a bridge."

"It does not substitute for the Soul making its own journey into the Godhead ... but it does make it more likely."

"The great cosmic joke, if you will, is that there is no place to go! Time and space, being an illusion, there really is no place to go and we discover that attention and focus are keys here. Coupled with Love and imagination, we may place our attention upon any plane if we are patient enough to follow the detailed instructions of the Spiritual Travelers, and begin to make the journey by his side."

"I appear to you to be an evolved Soul and shall I say a great Soul, but it is only the Great HURAY that deserves any praise for I am that I am. I am IT and I am HE. I am that I am and because of this, I exist in the pure worlds of Beingness, Seeingness and Isness."

"This sounds like a riddle does it not?"

AF: "Yes it does, Master."

Yaubl laughed.

YS: "Well it is. Until man experiences the high God worlds and establishes himself there through dying daily, he is little more than a gentle fool."

"So it is, we teach such Souls the gentle art of Tuza or Soul Travel."

"Things could not get any easier than this and yet, the Kal will put up a great fight. Actually, the Kal is really only a lower aspect of the ego of man manifesting as the fight between the little self and the God self. In the end, the God self always wins."

"The fight or, more accurately, process of purification or the separation of the God Self from the lower self may take millions or even billions of years to accomplish."

"VARDANKAR is a short cut to this process, and as such, represents a great act of compassion on the part of the HURAY towards Soul, who is a drop from ITS Great Ocean of Love and Mercy."

"Soul is destined to be a conscious co-worker with the HURAY."

"We may serve in our lower bodies, because we may dwell in the God-Worlds while serving here. Then our lower bodies become vehicles or tools, to be used and abused by the VARDAN and HURAY, for ITS Purpose."

"In the case of myself, my body is very old because this was determined necessary, in order to fulfill my spiritual mission at this time. Other VARDAN Masters, such as Paulji, may only last a short time in their respective lower bodies."

"It matters little except that, the will of the HURAY be followed out."

"Soul is eternal and only exists in the here and now. "

"God also exists, of course, in the here and now. To delay our journey to God is to deny our very divinity and is pure foolishness, and yet the Living VARDAN Master will seldom say anything, but just grant Souls their psychic space to make mistakes and learn their own lessons."

"Those who refuse the Master's help, or worse curse him, will have to suffer the consequences of spitting into the face of God."

"It is not God who really cares, but the individual may have to wait a long time before being given another opportunity for truth."

R.T: "Thank you!" Rebazar nodded graciously. "I wish to say that the Sound Current, of which we have talked about beforehand, is the second necessity. We have already covered it somewhat so we will move on to the initiation..."

Rebazar closed his eyes and remained silent.

Yaubl paused, his eyes open, as if gazing into some unseen world.

The vibrations coming out of these two beings was very powerful, and I felt a great sense of peace and Wisdom. Then Yaubl began to speak.

Y.S: "Most of this is very private, known only to the VARDANISTS who are initiated under the Living VARDAN Master. The whole movement of VARDANKAR is somewhat secret in nature. Man does not understand it, does not comprehend it. Although he does not even realize this but thinks, the whole works are a joke or false teachings. As Paulji said, 'he does not have the eyes to see nor the ears to hear."

"The initiations are given on both the inner and the outer. When one receives his or her second initiation, it's a direct link up with the VARDAN through the Master and the initiation itself. He is then given a secret word. He is forbidden from discussing his initiation except to perhaps say he received it, but must say nothing about what happened. This is known as the law of silence."

"To understand the initiation, we must understand the Audible Life Stream or VARDAN that flows out from the heart of HURAY in a descending wave and an ascending wave, much like a radio beacon moves out into the world and then reflects back and returns to its source. So it is the HURAY issues forth the great Audible Life Stream or VARDAN that sustains all. The VARDAN steps down through the various planes, lowering itself in vibration, and then upon reaching the bottom of creation, the physical universe, it returns as the ascending wave back to the very heart of HURAY in the Ocean of Love and Mercy."

"The initiation has to do with the very link-up, with this Audible Life Stream current of VARDAN."

"There is really little that can be said, except that, until Soul is linked through the initiation given by the Living VARDAN Master or one of his representatives, he is not connected strong enough or in a direct enough way, to overcome the mighty pull of the Kal force who pulls Souls down."

"One could almost say, that we must grab a hold of this ascending wave and let go of the descending or downward moving wave, and the true initiations give us this direct link."

"Until then, we are drifting and do not have the power or will, to move past the lower worlds of time and space."

"The spiritual exercises are the secret techniques given to VARDAN initiates through a series of discourses from the Master. There are also some exercises that may be given in books such as this. The Living VARDAN Master must be careful, as you know, to not give out too much of the secret teachings to those who are not under his protection and are not initiates on the path."

"One needs the inner protection and guidance of the Living VARDAN Master, and this level of commitment comes through taking on the path and true contemplation upon the VARDAN works. The discourses are written at a high vibratory rate that facilities the chela's spiritual growth. The discourses are not to be studied by anyone outside of VARDANKAR."

"As you know, the God Worlds chart shows the various planes and the words to be chanted for the different planes."

"One can call upon any of the VARDAN Masters for protection during their exercises, or at any time."

"This is really a subject that needs to be covered in more depth, but we are nearing the end of this discourse and I must leave."

AF: "Thank you Yaubl for coming."

YS: "May the blessings be!"

RT: "This ends this series of dialogues for now. We will pick up later on."

And with that, both Masters disappeared. I was exhausted and needed to rest. Perhaps they had sensed this.

8

WHO IS THE MASTER?

RT: "Today we are going to talk about who exactly is the Master."

"Many men argue about this. But there is really no question. There are lesser teachers who are not truly masters and then there is the Master: he who holds the Rod of Power. God, in ITS infinite wisdom has appointed at any one time, a true Spiritual Traveler and this Master is always, always picked by the HURAY for the purpose of acting as ITS representative here on Earth and all other planets to bring forth the message of VARDANKAR, namely that man can leave his body through the methods outlined and taught, and find Spiritual freedom by venturing into the Soul plane or ATMA region and beyond."

"All other so called Masters only lead to cosmic consciousness or planes below the Soul Plane, and therefore lesser realizations, and because of this there is no liberation, but only death and decay and life again, in an endless cycle of incarnations only temporarily stopped, by longer incarnations on the planes above the Physical, but below the Soul Plane."

"It is a fact that Soul's only goals should be to return to the Soul Plane, having found true Self Realization, and shed its lower bodies, and then as Soul progresses under the Masters, find true God Realization and become a conscious Co-worker and achieve Total Awareness."

"This is always Soul's goal although in the short run Soul may get distracted, ultimately this is where we are headed if we desire it."

"The true Master has nothing to do with competence nor physical or emotional qualities ... although he may be high on these, it has nothing to do with appearances. It is the Rod of Power and this Soul's job as the Living VARDAN Master that holds the key."

"This individual acts as the conduit for countless Souls to find the path via the Living VARDAN Master, the initiations, and the VARDAN or Audible Life Stream, and self-surrender to the inner, not outer, but inner Master. Do you understand me so far?"

AF: "Yes I think so ... but ..."

Rebazar looked at me intensely.

RT: "You are a new Margatma and it shows in your outer consciousness. This is one of the myths that man has: That the Master must be perfect in every way. This is unfortunately mythology! The Master is perfect on the inner planes from the Anami on up, but is imperfect at the lower levels from the Etheric on down. In his physical and astral bodies, the Master is a man just as you are a man. It is only in the Nuri Sarup or Soul body, also known of course as the Tuza, that the Master has perfection."

"He becomes the VARDAN of ITSELF in personalized form, for the purpose of bringing Souls back to God. He is the way shower."

"But how does one tell who the Master really is? Let alone what the Master really is?"

"I tell you this. Man must chant the sacred words such as HU and go into deep sincere contemplation. Then he shall know. Man must go inwardly with utter sincerity and a deep and burning love for God. Then, and only then, will he know who and what the Master is. Then he will follow whoever the true Master is, and know he is in the trusted hands of the VARDAN and is indeed worthy."

"Should you doubt this statement, you are in the mind and in the grasp of the Kal power. The only way to break this hold that the Kal has upon you is utter and complete faith in the Great Spirit or VARDAN, the Audible Life Stream. Then, as said previously, with total surrender, love and serenity, we ask the Master humbly for help in finding true spiritual liberation within this lifetime."

"The Great HURAY, through ITS agents, will tell anyone if they are sincere what to do, provided they are sincere and love God. However, many have little faith and, for them perhaps, they are not ready to find the true Master?"

"When I was the Margatma, the Living VARDAN Master, I did not care who joined me or who left me. For, I was with God at all times as I still am. Time and space, being an illusion, we all dwell in the arms of the HURAY but, this is not enough! We must become conscious of it, thus as Paulji stated, achieve Total Awareness not just in the lower worlds of time and space, but in all of God's many universes. This can only be done by becoming that for which we already are: The living breathing truth: The VARDAN of ITSELF."

Then I noticed Yaubl Sacabi appeared.

Y.S. "There is a rhythm about the sound current that Soul may come into harmony with. This is not a beat as in the beat

66

of a human heart ... no I say, it is that divine sound current, the Audible Life Stream carrying Soul onward, on its journey back to God."

"This cosmic current or VARDAN, returns back on the great returning wave we have spoken of before. But if one becomes totally absorbed in this sound, there is a secret vibration or rhythm that mesmerizes Soul so IT desires to stay in this state forever."

"The spiritual travelers will often yank a Soul gently or even forcefully out of their present state into a higher one, through the transcendence of this vibration from one rhythm onto another finer sound. Then all of a sudden, the Soul finds ITSELF in another world of light and sound. This can be done on virtually any plane."

"But generally, it is done when a Soul is practicing the spiritual exercises, and willing to demonstrate a degree of perfection in their desire to find truth, and a level of love and sincerity."

"It's like the snake that is enchanted by the piper's melody. The mind becomes still and the sound current puts Soul in the driver's seat where Soul surrenders to the great Audible Life Stream or VARDAN Sound Current. There is also a great light: Sometimes a sheet of white or yellow light, depending on the plane. This too vibrates, and Soul may begin to rock back and forth in consciousness."

"When a Soul finally re-enters the human body, they often do so with a jerking, as if jerked back into their physical bodies."

"They are aware that something has occurred but, often, do not know precisely what. If they are fortunate later on, they will know and remember more."

"The whole process is one of an awakening and spiritual unfoldment rather than a mental understanding or emotional development."

"The Master will see to it that the chela is progressing. But he must have the cooperation of the chela or student. If the chela refuses to follow the Master's instructions, then there is trouble and the chela may suffer needlessly."

"Some fall off of the path because they cannot surrender to the Master. These individuals may have gone as far as they can on the path but generally they are making a gigantic mistake leaving, for sooner or later, they will remember what has been happening in the dream state and during their waking life."

"They have been meeting with the various VARDAN Masters, and studying and being taken into certain states of consciousness … some higher than others."

"It is sad when a Soul fails to remember, but this is a part of the lower worlds and happens more then we can imagine."

"It is the temporal nature of the lower worlds and, this is the great danger that one may forget."

"One can travel into another plane but then entirely forget what happened. There must be some effort and sincerity otherwise the Kal will easily discourage the individual."

"I love you dearly and desire that you understand what has been happening, so that you do not fall or find yourself confused. You must have faith in the HURAY, the VARDAN and the ancient VARDAN Masters. All must have faith in the HURAY that IT will bring those who are sincere to the gates of heaven, if they will but submit in love to IT and desire IT above all else, instead of seeking the false truth through the whisperings of the space God's, such as the Kal and Brahmanda, who only offer them illusion or maya."

9

DYING DAILY

RT: "Let us begin, it is morning."

AF: "Yes Master."

R.T. "I wish to do a discourse on dying daily. This is a very important subject. Once Soul understands through contact with the spiritual travelers, that it can leave its body at will and travel to the various planes, including the Higher Planes beyond time and space, Soul begins to experience a certain level of joy and freedom."

"This freedom and joy is actually the Audible Life Stream or VARDAN making contact with him and ITS power is beyond measure. It is not the power of the Kal, which controls the lower universes, but an unselfish power that not only contains all Love, Wisdom, Power and Freedom but, allows man the freedom to move about upon ITS great wave to any and all universes of God in the blink of an eye."

"So great is this power that man cannot fathom it. And yet strangely he rejects it because it does not meet with his ideas about what a power should do for him. You see this power does not conform to his will in the lower worlds but has a will of ITS own: that of the VARDAN Stream. This mighty power, that sustains all, is so fine in vibratory rate that it, of itself, can only do God's will, and this will becomes our will for we and the great spirit of life, the Audible Life Stream, the VARDAN, the Holy Spirit, call it what you will; but this power uses us and, in a strange sense, we are IT and IT is us."

"You see, Soul by its eternal nature is this power. Of course, Soul is much more than this. Soul is cut out of the same cloth as God. You could say, with some accuracy, that Soul is a drop from the Ocean of Love and Mercy, that mighty dwelling place of the Supreme Being, the HURAY or God of ITSELF."

"So perhaps you see the necessity of dying daily during our spiritual exercises."

"We fear not death, for death is life and life is death. We do not dwell in the body except as a man drives his car."

"We use the body as a vehicle in order to carry out our earthly interactions at the various psychic and material levels; mainly at the astral and physical levels of existence. We do this and it is our duty to eventually learn to be conscious co-workers with the VARDAN and God or HURAY."

"But in order to be truly conscious, we must have awareness ... what is consciousness but awareness and the sublime presence of God in our lives."

"This is not an astral or emotional feeling, but a profound relationship with the Deity and with the Holy Spirit of VARDAN that issues out of God."

"This is not true, in a sense of the lower rulers, for they issue out dual energies and do not hold the truth; only a shadow of truth."

"They are like the field of opposites; alternating opposites of positive, negative and neutral forces: Good and evil, light and dark, love and hate, kindness and cruelty. This is where the

71

moral teachings of man springs from. The Kal makes social organizations, and social public opinions, and the mass consciousness of religions, and philosophies and dogma."

"The Kal places undue attention upon this world because it is the master, or ruler of this world and has no other. It is the Kal's job, as I have said before, to keep Soul within the lower worlds of matter, energy, time and space for as long as possible; and it is Soul's solemn duty to escape."

"This escape comes through the spiritual traveler and Soul's relationship with the Inner VARDAN Masters, in particular the Living VARDAN Master of the times."

"It is said that those who hate the Living VARDAN Master hate God and that those who love him love God. This is true for the Living VARDAN Master acts as a gateway and, it is through him that, all Souls escape in the quickest time form possible."

"This is not to say things are easy for Soul. But the way will be made if they learn to love the Living VARDAN Master."

"I speak mostly of the Inner Master; the outer Master is just a series of bodies that carry on the divine work of God. Much like any other lower bodies, they are subject to death, illness and so forth.

"The Inner Masters body is of the VARDAN! This and this alone! And his body is universal in nature for he holds the VARDAN Rod of Power, and is a conduit to take Souls back home to God within their lifetime, or the next."

"You may ask what this has to do with the subject of dying daily? It is simple really. There is nothing keeping man from leaving his body except his own stubborn nature and fear!

When one makes contact with the Living VARDAN Master, he has two choices. He may follow the Master, or he may not follow and reject the Master. This is entirely up to him."

"The Master will generally be patient with him to the extreme. There is no pressure. The individual must make his or her own decision, and the Master will stay clear and not interfere unless invited. Many, who are ready, have studied the high path of VARDANKAR during their past lives. They may not remember but this is generally so. Of course, VARDANKAR has had many names before. It is the unifying line of Masters, and methods they use that has remained for the most part, the same. The divine principle that gives clues."

"The Living VARDAN Master is the way shower."

AF: "Why was I chosen?"

RT: "Oh … yes, this is a great mystery!" Rebazar laughed.

AF: "Seriously, I do not feel like the most qualified."

RT: "The HURAY has ITS reasons and we simply carry out ITS will. I am not going to go into that now. But I will say this. For far too long, man has engaged in personality worship. He is always looking for a new being to worship or trying to figure out how to worship a man more, than he already is worshiping him."

"This worship has turned into a terrible disease. The Living VARDAN Master of the time frowns on this sort of thing because it disempowers Soul and traps them in their skulls, or at least within the Astral or emotional regions of time and space."

"You do have a propensity to get this message across. That it is the individual chela or student that is most important, for each and every one of them are Gods among other Gods, and we are all moving towards God's or HURAY's divine plan."

Yaubl Sacabi appeared as I sensed him before.

YS: "We cannot stop the river of God from bringing Souls back home to IT. IT demands it. That Soul should return to IT. Should we resist, there is always pain in the end. Maybe not right away, but there is always pain when we try and delay our spiritual progress or reunion with that which we already are, but have forgotten."

"The process of spiritual unfoldment is one of Realization. Not evolution. We are, as the mighty oak is, contained inside the acorn seed. There before us is the divine plan. We are Gods among other Gods as Rebazar Tarzs so aptly stated. This is not original in nature, but when philosophers say this, they do not understand the very nature of God nor the very nature of Soul, or who we really are. When they say we are Gods among other Gods, they are generally referring to illusion, to the lower bodies. They are talking about God as the Brahm or negative power, and they are seeing themselves as a physical and astral body, or ego or lower self, struggling to find control over its environment. This has nothing to do with anything, other than the negative worlds and men, trying to conquer their own perceived inadequacies."

"In this sense, they are not Gods among other Gods, but you would say more like fools among other fools. I do not mean to malign, but man has been appalling in his ignorance of truth."

"When the Living VARDAN Master speaks of this topic, he is referring to the HURAY who dwells in the Ocean of Love and Mercy far above duality. He is referring also to our true God self Soul, who is, you could say poetically of course, a drop from this Ocean of Love and Mercy, therefore because it is cut of the same cloth as God, although the drop is not the whole of the ocean, the drop is identical in substance as we are identical as our true self to God, and yet paradoxically; because we are not the whole, we are not identical of course, because if we were identical to God, we would be God and this is not possible! So thus lies the paradox that cannot be solved with the mind, but only through Tuza Travel into the high, high worlds where dwells the great HURAY."

AF: "Yes Yaubl, there seems to be a great confusion over what exactly is Soul and what Soul is not. It seems man confuses his astral body or light body with Soul."

RT: "This has always been true. It is illusion at its worst and holds Souls in bondage. Just as bad, is for Soul to believe it is its mental body."

YS: "One, as you all know must go into those regions high above the lower worlds to truly understand even a small part of what we are speaking of today. Thus we finally get to the topic of dying daily.

"What we are doing is leaving our body and traveling with the Master into the various worlds and golden wisdom temples of VARDAN in order to acquire certain spiritual realizations that cannot be reached through books but must come directly from contact with that Cosmic Sound Current known as the VARDAN."

"This Audible Life Stream or VARDAN comes directly from the Godhead, but it is not God of itself but the spirit of God."

"IT contains all. All Love, all Wisdom, all Power, all Freedom and beyond all. It is that which sustains all and is the totality of all. Within it is contained all Beingness, Seeingness, Knowingness and direct perception. It is unlimited and cannot be put inside any box nor defined other than to say that it is undefined."

"The qualities listed, are only a part of IT but never the whole.

"All perception, in fact all consciousness and awareness comes out of this mighty river, that flows out from the HURAY and ITS Ocean of Love and Mercy, and extends out in all directions.

"As IT moves, if you can call it moving for IT is beyond all time and space, but I use the word moves for lack of a better word. As it issues forth, IT cannot be stopped nor stifled in any way. But ITS vibrations are lowered as it enters each succeeding lower plane. This is the vastness or expansiveness of the HURAY in action. It must expand and move outwardly into this world.

"Most men make the mistake of thinking that they see the whole picture or understand the very nature of consciousness and of life, or at least they believe they are close to this.

"This is not true! All one can do is expand and learn to dwell in these high, high, worlds. Just because we experience a great amount of divine wisdom, power, love and freedom; just because we have God Realization, we cannot be so vain as to think we are the whole. And yet paradoxically we are the whole!

"Do you understand? Do you comprehend? What I am saying is simply this. Man, no matter who he is, will never fully realize God but only by surrender, does he even begin."

"The spiritual travelers have seen the face of God, and God

or HURAY has commanded them to give certain chosen Souls the opportunity to return to IT if they choose."
"Not in the future, but in the here and now."

"There is always a plus factor; never an end. There are countless planes upon planes and beings upon beings. The universes of God are beyond comprehension and yet they are not beyond experience."

"While it is true that Seeing, Knowing and Being exist in the high heavens, and that we know all things and have direct perception beyond mind, we must never be so vain as to believe we have reached the ultimate state of awareness. And yet by reaching these great heights, we are transformed or born anew, and have reached a new evolutionary scale: that of the God man."

"We are no longer the fool but a God Realized and fully conscious being who, simultaneously dwells in both the lower worlds and higher worlds at the same time, and can serve using our lower bodies as vehicles or tools to interact with those Souls, who desire to escape and reach Self and God Realization within their respective lifetimes."

"So the act of dying daily is not something to fear. It is like the caterpillar who is transformed into the beautiful butterfly. No man is an island unto himself. All must learn to be humble before God and to surrender. Then the spiritual travelers can come into our lives and make it bright, through the teachings of VARDANKAR."

"There is no need to give up your job or family. We can do our spiritual exercises for as little as 30 minutes a day. Many find they desire to do this twice daily: once in the morning and another time in the evening. But whatever schedule the chela chooses, he must be sincere and honest with himself. Does he really desire God or is he looking for God's favor so he can accumulate the things of this world for his own benefit? Does he see God as a sort of Santa Claus, or does he truly love enough to make that sacred journey back to the Godhead, and take his rightful place as a conscious co-worker?"

"Does he love God so much, that he is willing to listen and follow the instructions of the Living VARDAN Master, who God has appointed in order the help Souls reach IT?"

"Or is he so jaded in arrogance and conceitedness, that he does not believe that any man could possibly know that much more than himself?"

"Is he willing to let go of dogma, preconceived notions and attachments because of his great love to find truth? Or would he rather watch TV and entertain his body and emotions? Or attend some religious organization where his thinking is done for him, and he does not have to be responsible for his own state of consciousness nor deal with the contemplation upon truth."

"I tell you this young man, I am very old and yet look at me. I do not appear more than thirty, thirty-five, do I not?"

AF: "Yes you do!"

YS: "Why do I bring this up? Because I have been around and seen many things over the years; far too many, so called students of truth, deceive themselves by being far too cavalier with the Master. They fail to see or believe what the Master says and thus are not just skeptical, but fail to follow out the instructions to the letter. Do not do this!"

"Let me tell you a story. There were two farmers in ancient times. One followed all the instructions given him to the letter,

78

and was careful to make sure he understood them to the best of his ability, so that he could follow them. There were times when, frankly, he did not understand why he was doing certain things, but he did them anyway because he respected the fact that those who told him, had grown many crops for many, many years and knew what they were talking about."

"The second farmer, or more accurately would-be-farmer, had a different idea. He would follow most of what he was instructed to do. But if he did not understand something or felt it was a waste of time, he would play with the idea of skipping that particular instruction. What harm could come of this he thought. Why, I bet many of these instructions for growing crops are wrong anyway."

"And so it was."

"At the end of the season, the first famer who followed the instructions, prepared the seed the way it was supposes to be prepared, prepared the soil the way it was supposed to be prepared and did everything he was supposed to do, had a great crop and counted himself as a most fortunate man indeed!"

"The second farmer did not do nearly as well. Because he skipped certain steps in order to try and save time and money, he found his crop was less than half of the first farmer. Because of this, he and his family suffered."

"But strangely, this experience was not enough to stop him from doing the very same thing next year. This time, he chose to ignore different steps and do some he did not do before. He had, you see, blamed the whole affair on inferior soil. It was the soil's fault, not his own."

"The next year again, the studious farmer has a great crop but, this time, the foolish farmer had no crop at all! It had all died on him for some mysterious reason."

"He demanded an explanation! Why had he failed!"

"He thought, maybe someone had poisoned his soil? Or cursed his land? Or perhaps the seeds he was sold were not good!"

"He stormed into a place where many elderly farmers were eating and drinking and demanded an explanation. Why had his crop died!! He demanded to know!"

"The elders asked him questions. But it soon became apparent that this man had changed everything. He had recreated the ancient methods of farming that had worked for hundreds of years, and replaced them with his own version. To make it even worse, he could not even remember exactly what he had done. When pressed, he said he could not remember."

"Eventually, he sold his land at a great loss and left the area, claiming that someone had sold him bad seed, and it was not his fault. He said the town was a bad town and blamed everything on others, instead of realizing he had created the whole mess, by his inability to be humble and listen carefully."

"This is often the relationship of a bad chela to the Master. It's not that the chela is a bad person; he is just not willing or able to follow the instructions of the Master."

"I have encountered this so often that it is almost sickening. Or at least, it use to be until I become more detached about the whole thing. What I learned is this. That one must let his chelas make their own mistakes but at the same time point out the pitfalls, and correct methods the chela needs to use, in order to find success."

"Some will not go far while others will. It generally comes down to, how strong is their desire for God vs their affinity for their ego or little self. If the little self is stronger than their desire for God, then there will be lots of trouble ahead for them, until the ego gets more under Soul's control.

"This is a hard path to follow so the Master tries to teach true humility. True humility is not putting the Master on a pedestal and begging at his feet, but taking responsibility and yet being humble and listening. The Living VARDAN Master is the way shower. He does not demand worship in any way, shape or form; he only desires that his chelas listen to him when he speaks and that they carefully weigh his words."

10

A FIRE FOR GOD

As I pondered the previous words of the great Yaubl Sacabi, I realized a strange thing. Here I was the Master and yet there was so much I did not understand. Yes I had been to the God Worlds but it seemed that the path of VARDANKAR runs deeper than any man can fathom. That it is true that there is always a plus factor and that there was much I needed to know.

YS: "You are wondering?" Yaubl smiled gently."

AF: "Yes."

YS: "Spirituality is not what man thinks it is. It is the willingness to partake of that consciousness that comes out of the HURAY at the very highest level we are capable, but it is more than this."

"It is the willingness to surrender and work with what we have at hand, even when it is not what we had hoped to work with. We have a mind and lower bodies and we are, in a sense, forced to deal with them. Eventually, they change as the individual particles of light and sound flow through us; they vibrate our lower bodies and can change them. But this is generally a slow process, although, there have been times in recorded history when instant changes occur so violently, that they are known by humans as Divine Miracles!"

"But we must let the HURAY use us and not demand we control the situation; but we may change things within the law of love. The great law that as long as we follow, supersedes all other laws. But it is not an emotional love but a divine love. We must do everything in the name of the HURAY, VARDAN and Master and we must surrender if there is to be any hope of humility."

AF: "Thank you."

YS: "There is a fire. It burns deep inside of Soul. I do not speak of the astral body but of Soul ITSELF. The astral body appears, as if it's made of millions of stars, and it is also known by some as the light body. The fire for God ignites a passion or desire to return to Soul's source, God ITSELF!"

"This fire is caught rather than taught. In fact, this whole movement of VARDANKAR is caught rather than taught!"

"Once this fire begins, it will consume all in its path in order for Soul to reach the Godhead. First it will begin to destroy anything that is holding Soul back from God. The ego will suffer and cry out in pain and anguish, for the ego is afraid it will get lost and so generally rebels against the Master."

"The fire of God is actually Soul's burning love for God and it must burn brightly, for in order to overcome the obstacles of these lower worlds there is much pain, and in order to make it, Soul must desire God above all else: Truth above all else."

"One of the jobs of the Margatma, the Living VARDAN Master as you know, is to fan the flames of this fire of God or of the VARDAN. This fire of the VARDAN begins to burn brighter and brighter until it begins to consume the lower self only leaving that part of the lower self that Soul needs in order to complete its spiritual mission here on Earth before departing permanently to whatever plane Soul has earned or desires to stay."

"Soul must serve God if it is to find immortality. The sun must shine upon all and Soul is far mightier than any sun."

"But Soul must desire God, and this fire of God is the burning love and compulsion to return back to the Godhead."

"Books will not squelch the fire of God. Mere words will not help."

"It takes the words and writings of the Margatma, the Living VARDAN Master, to begin to satisfy this hunger for God, but even this by itself will not work for long."

"The individual will find that the Master is giving him instructions on how to return to the Godhead! This and little more can be gotten out of the teachings. Once one has returned; all Love, Wisdom, Power and Freedom are given unto them and, in a sense, they become a law unto themselves. But this law must tie into the law of Love otherwise that Soul will fall mighty far."

"Many have fallen because they forgot the law of Love. That we must give good-will to all beings upon all worlds and that this universal law comes from the very fabric of the HURAY'S consciousness and the Ocean of Love and Mercy."

"Actually, we never serve our fellow man; only the HURAY, VARDAN and Master. We are not interested in serving human embodiments for they are of the Kal. However, we may give aid and comfort. Perhaps feeding a homeless man or giving advice to an elderly person if the VARDAN so directs our actions. We do these things in the name of the HURAY, the Master and the VARDAN. These are karmaless acts of kindness. We do not make good karma from them nor bad karma. We are simply transcending karma and living the karmaless life."

"We do this through Grace or the law of love, through surrender and most important through doing everything in the name of the Master, the HURAY and the VARDAN. Any questions?"

AF: "Sometimes I find my body out of balance. What am I doing wrong?"

YS: "This is a strange question. You cannot possibly know the answer until you step aside in the ego self and view from the detached viewpoint. The problem is, you are too close to the problem and all wrapped up in it, as you see these things as trouble, or a problem or series of problems. Until you become detached, you will not see clearly what is happening."

"It's often best to ignore a so called problem and focus on what we want. But if we are wise, like I said before, we will only desire to serve God as conscious agents of IT and learn to completely surrender to IT and do everything in ITS Name. Then we are living the karmaless life, as you are beginning to learn."

"I have to say that anyone can be used as a channel for the VARDAN, but most people only get in their own way. This is the works of the Kal power, who does not desire the VARDAN to enter this world, but tries to crowd out the VARDAN through the use of hypnotic diversion and distraction, mainly keeping Soul's attention away from truth and God, and on mundane things like ideas, emotions and the physical life."

"If we master the art of attention, and learn to place it upon God and service to God, then all will be well; that is provided we get out of the way and not try and control the situation too much. We need to let go from the ego standpoint, and be so aware of the Higher Worlds that we consciously dwell in them while we operate a body here on Earth!"

"This is my secret, as it is the secret of all true VARDAN Masters. You are learning to do this and have done it. But as you practice this, it eventually does not stop. It becomes the norm and you are much more even keel."

"Your present illness will pass slowly over time as you clear your inner channels and get the message out to the public for there are some on this Earth world who desperately need to know this information and find this path. Most will not want to give you the time of day but this should be of no concern for these are the unready Souls who don't have the ears to hear or the eyes to see and frankly you are better off without them joining as you know."

"Returning to the subject of a Fire for God: this fire must start like all fires. It starts in the heart of man as he undergoes many lifetimes. At first man is fearful and confused, but begins to enjoy the process of incarnating. Other times he is terrified with fear. He becomes frantic or desperate for some form of relief from pain, then finds pleasure and gets lost in the five passions of the mind. He seeks revenge; then seeks the kindness and compassion of a woman or mother, sister or brother; perhaps a friend. He wanders around, wages war, fights for peace, becomes a prostitute, a priest, a beggar, lawyer, doctor, farmer, blacksmith, carpenter, seamstress, king, prince, fisherman, gay, lesbian, strong, weak, retarded, genius, and so on and so on."

"He wields power over others and often abuses such power. He creates karma, works off karma and finds himself incarnating with various Souls in his Soul group. He will, for example, incarnate as a husband with another Soul, then they may switch places and he is now a she. Or he may be the husband, then the friend. His wife may incarnate as his brother

DIALOGUES WITH THE MASTERS

in another lifetime, or he her sister. This goes on and on, lifetime after lifetimes. At times, he may earn enough good karma to spend some time in some Astral paradise before returning to Earth. He may earn good karma and spend it on being wealthy and healthy and living a life of luxury ... then his next life may be one of poverty and hardship. He may have a lifetime as a Japanese sumo wrestler, and the next, a geisha girl. Followed by an American Indian male with one leg missing. There seems to be no end in sight to this but, this is where the spiritual travelers come in."

"VARDANKAR is not the only way back to God, but it is the most direct. If man truly understood this: that he can learn to die daily, and leave his body and venture with the help of the Living VARDAN Master into the high worlds of VARDAN, and find spiritual liberation, and God consciousness and God Realization, he would stop all this travel and revolutions upon the 'wheel of 84.'"

"The fire of God starts as the most minute of sparks. It may be drowned in an ocean of tears, buried under a mountain of Earth."

"The Soul may undergo the cave of fire that burns him, drown in the depth of the ocean of the Kal's negativity, and generally suffer for more time than most men care to fathom."

"At some point, they are chosen by the HURAY to return. But they must answer a call first. As the saying goes, "Many are called but few are chosen." Most reject the Master and God in favor of a space God who grants them wishes like a genie. The funny part is, this space God gives them little and asks that their very Souls be given onto him. This space God is, of course, the Brahm, the very negative power or universal mind power, itself."

"The fire of God does not burn brightly enough for most to even find the Master and join VARDANKAR."

"For those who join the Master, the tests are not over but have just begun: they must be bold, adventurous, cunning and resourceful, if they are to reach the Higher Worlds and gain spiritual liberation within their lifetime, and perhaps even reach True spiritual Mastership and join the order of the Bourchakoun."

"It is time we rest now. We will take up more of the study of VARDANKAR later today."

11

DETACHMENT

YS: "Why are you so discouraged?"

AF: "As you know my health is not ... well it does not seem too good right now."

YS: "You must live for the moment. Yes it's true you need to take care of your physical body. Did you think things would be easy for you?"

AF: "No, but there are times, Master, when I'm not sure how much longer I will be on this Earth. Just today I was wondering if I would translate." (Another word for die)

YS: "I am very old as you know. But it is not because I am afraid of death; only that I have things to do in this world and therefore I need a physical vehicle to carry on. Perhaps you need one as well?"

AF: "Yes, but it may not last much longer."

YS: "This is a topic for another time, in private. What I want to impart to you today is the absolute essential nature of detachment in VARDANKAR. When a man is attached, he cannot control himself. He is out of control and stuck in whatever present state of consciousness he is dwelling in at the time."

"Detachment allows us to leave our body and follow the Master into the other worlds. It allows us also to work for the universal good as a conscious channel for God, even when conditions are not ideal and the Kal may be attacking us left and right."

"We don't really need anything in this world, therefore we are in this world but not of this world. We become disinterested in life, and yet we are so interested in God or HURAY, and following the laws of Spirit, that we become spirit or the VARDAN of ITSELF."

"We always were the VARDAN. It's just we have become unconscious of this fact. It's not enough to know it intellectually. We must feel IT and be IT but, most of all, we must be in the elevated state of being Spirit of ITSELF and Soul, being identical with spirit, we are simply being our self. Not the little self, but the True Self Soul which, as we have pointed out over and over again, is simply a drop from the Ocean of Love and Mercy. But this drop or Soul must become conscious, and we do not become conscious by thinking or feeling, nor reading nor doing things; no, no; we become conscious by the very act of BEINGNESS; of simply BEING in that state where we ARE."

"Now this may sound, to some, like some mental play on words, but it is not. Only those who have experienced the God Worlds of VARDAN truly understand what I am speaking of here and now!"

"We enter the worlds of BEINGNESS! Seeing, Knowing and BEINGNESS. Or BEING!"

"See! Only Out-of-Body Tuza Travel can do this for us, that is, provided we are catapulted into the ecstatic states high above the lower worlds. And this is best done through the surrender to a true Spiritual Traveler and VARDAN Master under his watchful eye."

"This is so ridiculously simple that most men cannot believe it. The Kal power has so well brainwashed man into thinking that he is a body, emotions and mind, that man cannot even separate his components and understand that he is Soul."

"Man does not even know what the word Soul means and confuses it with his astral or mental body! See…"

Yaubl looked at me with his brown eyes luminescent. There was something about them and him that I knew at once, that he was reaching and drawing me into the high, high, worlds of God."

YS: "Do you see that perception cannot work if man is attached, and suffers from attachment?"

"When one is attached to something, they are bound and enslaved unto it. This is okay, if Soul desires to stay in these lower worlds for thousands or even millions of years, but if Soul desires God, Soul must go and find God or the HURAY, and the HURAY cannot be found in the mundane, the social, in books, the singing of hymns, or in church or temple. The HURAY cannot be found through the doing of good works nor the worship and adoration of IT. The HURAY does not need man's praises; only that he return to it, and in order to do this, man must become detached to this world."

"Ever ask yourself this question? Why does man incarnate over and over again for millions of years, when he could be, instead, dwelling in the bliss of God?"

"Because he is attached. He is attached to his need for self-punishment. He is attached to the things of this world: his woman, his money, his property, his friends, his social standing, his art, his skill, his religion, his community; his ideals and belief systems are all in place to bind him to these worlds!"

"Ever notice how most men cling to their ideals and bad habits to the point of being willing to kill to defend them?"

"Never argue with someone who does not wish to change, unless you want a dagger or sword thrust into you!"

"Never! Man does not want truth. Man does not want to give up on his attachments nor his lies, his petty religions and beliefs, his dogma and superstitions, his space God that he petitions for help in all manner of his life; including the gain of material wealth, the providing of food, shelter, clothing, social ties, health and the like."

"Man does not want God; he wants a Santa Claus, a sort of grotesque genie who will grant him a long series of wishes so that man can attempt to control his universe, because he is afraid and envious of his fellow men who have more good karma then he."

"It is only the very few who desire God above all else. Remember this the next time someone refuses your blessings."

"He does not want them. He would sooner receive $100 dollars than spiritual truth. He does not want God; he wants the trappings of this world such as sex, emotional happiness, wealth, power, the admiration of his fellow man, human love, social standing and excellent health."

"There is nothing wrong with these things; only that they are poor replacements for God indeed!"

"They are not truth; only dim reflections of the Kal's power."

"The Kal can and does provide man with endless amusements: sex, money, fame, social standing, admiration, human love, accomplishments galore, and even intellectual and emotional epiphanies."

"All of this does not replace the Great HURAY. It is not even Self Realization; only a shadow of self. Not even close to truth, but an illusion that mesmerize Souls into a sleep-like state or slumber."

"Man has a disease and that disease is reincarnation and unconsciousness to God, the VARDAN power and the Master."

"Man will never find happiness in this world over the long haul; only the alternating realities of duality: he swings back and forth from love to hate, mountains to valleys, sickness to health, poverty to prosperity. This is because the nature of the Kal or negative power or illusion in the lower worlds, is temporal and one of opposing opposites: man and woman, darkness and light, death and rebirth."

"If one desires pain and pleasure in a countless, alternating field of darkness; if one desires to live in the dark shadow of truth, where little light filters in, like in a dark cave with a small crack that lets in just enough air and light to barely see and breathe, then man may choose to stay in these lower worlds and fend for himself."

"He may try and help his fellow man but he is weak and feeble in consciousness. Without the vitality of the VARDAN and Master, man cannot find truth. There is a Spiritual vitality that I am speaking of here, a spiritual awakening."

"It does not occur except through the study and application

of VARDANKAR, the Ancient Science of Out-of-Body Tuza or Soul Travel."

"Man is like the fool who trades his Soul for a loaf of bread and a wooden nickel."

12

TEMPTATION

YS: "Hello Allen. Today I am going to talk about Temptation, among other subject matters. You are wondering why I am giving these dialogues with you, along with Rebazar Tarzs? It is this. We need to get the message out to the world and so we are using you, as you are the Margatma, the Living VARDAN Master, and it is your job. It is an irony isn't it that few understand. Why it is that imperfect human beings can be used as channels for the HURAY, in this world to uplift man spiritually?"

"But who else could God use? It seems that those who appear most perfect are not and those who appear least perfect are."

"In other words God or the HURAY does not really care about the petty standards by which men judge one another. It only cares about ITS will and Souls returning to IT and becoming citizens of the higher worlds and conscious agents and Co-workers. Nothing else. So the human standards mean nothing. The ideals of man, again, mean nothing. All appearance means nothing. It is rare for any Soul to be willing to serve. Most want something for their trouble but as you painfully realize, God can only give eternal life in ITS service, which is the greatest gift one can have: that of serving IT throughout eternity and being ITS agent and co-worker. What more could there be to life than this?"

"I say unto you that, do not be deceived by the liars and cheats of this world. They are like the proverbial vampire who will suck your psychic and spiritual blood. They will try and convince you that they know more than you and then, that you must follow them and do as they say. But upon further examination they know little or nothing about God, for they have not seen ITS face nor do they know of the VARDAN sound current, nor the light. They sell people on being like them and acting like them and this is sad because these individuals are not spiritual."

"God can offer you nothing but God. That connection with the forces, or more accurately, the presence of the Audible Life Stream which contains all Love, Wisdom, Power and Freedom in ITS voice, along with every other trait of a positive nature."

"I am beating around the bush here for the VARDAN is not a thing! IT simply IS. IT has ALL of this but IT is not THIS."

"These are only minute aspects of IT. To try and define IT without pause is foolish, for no matter how we try and define IT, whether that's through the observations of ITS LOVE, ITS POWER, ITS FREEDOM or ITS WISDOM , these are just aspects of a much greater reality; that of the consciousness that emanates from the very heart of God. What can one say about God or the HURAY? What can one say about the VARDAN, that is the Audible Life Stream or sound current that emanates from ITS mighty Ocean of Love and Mercy and sustains all Souls and all Worlds into eternity and beyond eternity?"

"We may try and define IT but IT is indefinable."
"However, we must try in our pitiful words and gestures to

articulate that which can only be experienced. Why? Why bother to put into words the indescribable?"

"Simply for this reason and this reason alone."

"The spiritual travelers must make man see his follies and do an about face. I am not talking here about all of mankind, but the individual Soul who is caught in illusion."

"We, as Masters, must strike up the imaginations of our chelas and of the world itself, in order that those who are ready can practice the techniques that, if practiced, will facilitate a new state of awareness …that of Total Consciousness, Total Awareness and Total Surrender to that which simply is: the VARDAN and ultimately God or HURAY."

"Then Soul becomes that which it always was: the VARDAN."

"It is not so much that Soul becomes this VARDAN, but that Soul realizes IT and this means Tuza or Soul travel to ITS Source and from there, the partaking of IT."

"Do I make myself clear here? We cannot partake of music if we do not listen. We cannot partake of the great cosmic power unless we are located in the center of that which is us. We are this great VARDAN as the individual expression of that which cannot be expressed except through drops of ITSELF, namely Souls who become God Realized or at the very least Self Realized."

"But before this can take place, the Soul must make the upward ascent by leaving the human body and venturing, with the aid of the Master, into these high, high, worlds."

"Meditation will not work for this because it is far too

passive in nature. Meditation is of the mind of man. At best it will tune one into the causal or mental plane ... but mostly the astral or even lower."

"Meditation is where man waits for something or some consciousness to descend into his physical body."

"This does not generally work, and those who have some success are not really meditating at all, but leaving their bodies to some degree and having some sort of experience."

"Meditation has been a dismal failure for man because it is passive and is of the Kal or negative power."

"Man must practice the spiritual exercises of VARDANKAR and discover clever techniques of leaving his body and venturing into the various worlds of God if he wants any hope of spiritual liberation within his respective lifetime."

"We now move to the main topic, that of temptation."

"Temptation is defined as the process of doing something we know in our heart is against us, and yet we do it anyway, out of some desire that is stronger than our sense of right and wrong."

"The only real moral path that anyone can follow is the path of Love, or more accurately, the Law of Love, as practiced by the VARDAN Masters."

"But this is so different than the love practiced by most men. Even Jesus did not truly practice the correct kind of love, although he attempted to; he failed."

"The true meaning of right and wrong is totally different than what man has been taught."

"Good and evil are strange in nature. Good means to follow a path that does not delay one on their journey back to the Godhead. Evil is that which delays one on their path or delays another Soul on ITS path back to God."

"Remember this is all God cares about ... that man returns to IT and becomes a conscious co-worker and useful citizen of the God worlds. Then man usually stays for a certain time period to serve in these lower worlds before permanently retiring into the higher worlds where he, in pure Soul form, performs some sort of universal work in conscious co-workership with the HURAY."

"This may be any number of tasks, and each Soul is special, and has its own interests and inclinations. Each Soul may specialize in particular areas of service, and this is what makes us so unique even though we are all Souls, and drops from the Ocean of Love and Mercy, the dwelling place of the HURAY."

"So now things are coming together on this discourse. You see where temptation comes in. Temptation is man's dark desire to delay his journey back to God for some perceived benefit: usually the dubious benefit of enjoying the things of the Kal."

"The funny part of all of this is that man does not really have to give up the things of this world; he only has to become detached from them. He can, for instance, enjoy a good meal. He can make love with his wife. He can laugh and joke around, even travel and enjoy the things of this world if that is his desire. God does not care whether man enjoys life or not, and certainly does not look down on anyone who does!"

"But what man needs to learn is detachment. To be just as happy eating a tuna fish sandwich as a gourmet meal. Then if he chooses the gourmet meal, God does not care and he may enjoy it."

"The five passions of the mind are normal functions of the mind that are out of control. For example, making love to one's wife does not have to be forsaken, unless the individual no longer wishes to do this sort of thing. But God certainly does not care either way! But if one begins to become controlled by sex to the point of excess, then it becomes a passion. The same with the eating of rich foods. We may eat them if we choose and again God does not care. But if we over-eat on them, and gain weight and become sick, we are engaging in gluttony which is a child of lust."

"Man needs to have some sort of ego while in this world. The ego is the "I" or that which separates the individual from the group."

"Ego is the little self or lower personality aspects and is necessary while Soul dwells in a human body. If one did not have some form of "I" or ego, they could not function in this world, and may starve to death, or be unable to look out for their own physical and other needs."

"However, when ego is taken to excess, it turns into vanity."

"For the record, the five passions or perversions of the mind are Lust, Greed, Vanity, Anger and Attachment."

"The yogis and others who claim we must give up all for God, are not really correct. God does not want our money nor does God care about our sex life, our dietary habits, what we eat, drink, or whether we work in a factory, or sell shoes, or are a Doctor, or are the King of England for that matter."

(Yaubl smiled as if amused.)

"You see, we must develop detachment; not become martyrs.

"But man does not understand this and thinks that his space God will fulfill his wishes. Or that science or religion, or working hard at his job, or his family will somehow make his life right and he will find happiness."

"This may be true in the short run, but not in the long run. Only God and returning to IT will make man complete and fulfill his divine purpose. This is not some pie in the sky theory, but proven out through countless experiences of Souls, who made the journey themselves."

"The VARDAN Masters have been with man for longer than man can remember, because man is always given the opportunity to return to God, but man spits in the face of the Spiritual Travelers, and only desires to partake of his senses and emotional feelings, much like some animal out in the woods."

"This is why the VARDAN Masters may appear scornful of man's cavalier attitude about life. For they know that Soul undergoes almost countless incarnations and that this attitude is one of great foolishness."

"Still for the most part, few will listen to the spiritual travelers.

"First of all, they do not believe them! Unless a Master can multiply fish or get out of handcuffs and a straightjacket while riding on a motor cycle, they don't believe he is a Master. What these individuals are looking for is physical proof and paranormal activities."

"The Master will generally refuse to put on a show because it's against spiritual law to try and get a student through miracles."

"Most do not have the eyes to see nor the ears to hear. Worst of all, most will not even listen. They reject the Master's words almost from the moment he opens his mouth or they read the first paragraph."

"The Kal or negative power has man well trained in the art of materiality and false values. Man thinks in terms of humanity, social ties, philosophies, religions, scholarly learning and books, emotions such as anger, joy, Love and hate."

"He looks at his life as a sort of Shakespearean play where he is the main actor on stage and this is exciting for him. To play his part well and then he may have the cheers of the crowd, bravo!! bravo!!"

"But this is a sad and empty existence for man. No matter whether he plays the King, Queen, Great Warrior, noble Pope or Priest or Priestess; whether he plays the man who saves the city or burns it to the ground, man shall not be happy for long."

"It is said that the HURAY has planted a seed inside of man; that he may never find eternal and true happiness until he returns to the Godhead of his father, the HURAY, and takes his rightful place in heaven."

"Man cannot find happiness through illusion or the things of this world. Nor through emotions, no matter how much rush he experiences for his woman or she for her man. No matter how much man is touched in the heart by a young and tender baby in his or her arms. No matter how much love man finds in this world, it by itself will not make him happy for long. It only increases the longing for God or HURAY, and in the end man must return to IT. Then, he may truly serve God and through service to God as a conscious co-worker, he brings great upliftment to mankind. Not necessarily in the form of material upliftment but, spiritual upliftment."

"So you see, we have come full circle here. Man was never meant to be an island onto himself, but on the other hand, he must reach a degree of spiritual perfection that defies his lower self, for man is never his lower self. The eternal Self Soul, or the Eternal God self Soul shall not rest until IT has reached the true Realization of the HURAY and, then and only then, will Soul truly graduate and find eternal happiness."

"This does not mean everything will be well in the lower worlds. In fact, any Soul who consciously serves the HURAY instead of the Kal or negative power, will find that the Kal will make every attempt to destroy him, in order to prevent the spiritual liberation of other Souls from happening."

"These lower worlds are a warring universe!"

"But have no fear. The HURAY has set up this perfect system for the education of Soul and none may interfere."

"The Spiritual Travelers must grant man freedom to choose his own path. And so, they stand by watching from afar for, they know most are not yet ready but will be, when the time is right."

"The two questions all beings must ask themselves is: One. Am I willing to listen to what the Living VARDAN Master has to say? Two. Am I willing to experiment and try and prove to myself whether what the Master is saying is real or not?"

"This is all the VARDAN Masters have ever asked for from the world. And yet, so few are willing to even go this far. They are so filled with dogma and cherished beliefs and opinions that they cannot hear a word. They only see contradictions with their own foolish belief systems and dogma."

"The Living VARDAN Master can do little or nothing for these individuals but wait. It may be thousands of incarnations before they are ready to listen and act upon his words."

"Even those who join him are not out of the woods yet. They may leave him for greener grass … so they believe. There are so many gurus and masters who are claiming easy street for the students; that their students can have everything they desire!"

"This is the worst sort of salesmanship and reeks of materiality and is a con game at its most deceitful."

"Why in heaven's name would God care whether you drove a beat up old car or a brand new one? Or for that matter, whether you took the bus to work or drove a Rolls Royce!"

"Even if God did care, what difference would it really make?"

"These individuals have not even spent the time to analyze their ideas and beliefs long enough to realize how foolish they are."

"And even for those who hold so called higher ideals. We find that the Kal power has many servants. The Kal wants man to remain in the lower worlds of time and space and uses its channels to help him with his mission of enslavement. Those Kal channels who speak of brotherly love and helping one another; if you listen closely what they are saying, is to stay in the lower states of Kal or time, space and the universal mind, and find happiness in these lower states."

"These people may or may not mean well, but they are certainly not enlightened nor do they understand anything above the Etheric. To be truthful, most are caught in the Astral Plane influences and are no higher than the mid to high astral world."

"They preach about doing good works, loving your neighbor, finding God ... which they believe is Jot Niranjan or the Brahm, although they won't use those names. They will call the God of the lower worlds, Alah, Brahm, Bramanda, Jehovah, Lord God, The Power, The way, Our heavenly Father, Yahweh and countless other names, but they are referring to these lower vibratory planes, the universal mind worlds and generally the astral worlds as if they are the heavenly kingdom!"

"Yes it's true, as you know that the astral and casual plane is filled with splendid cities of light, and many large buildings, and magnificent and impressive beings to see. But all of this is not even remotely close to the Great HURAY in ITS Ocean of Love and Mercy that exists beyond M.E.S.T. (matter, energy, space, time). That exists far beyond thought and is untouchable except via the Spiritual Exercises, and the practice of leaving one's body and traveling into these exalted states of consciousness, with aid of the True Masters who have already gone before you!"

"So you see. Illusion is necessary so that those Souls who are not ready can amuse themselves but, it is also a sad fact that man suffers so much when he could end his suffering, by simply loving God and being more sincere in his efforts for truth, and listen to the spiritual travelers who try and give him truth. Not the watered down lies that religions and philosophies give man, but the real truth and the proper application of Tuza or Soul travel, to finding spiritual liberation through reaching the God worlds, and not through the false teachings of moral perfectionism, which as you know does not work nor does it touch God where IT dwells far above such concerns as, whether you starch your underwear or not, or whether you have an argument with your spouse or not."

Yaubl seemed a bit excited as he made his point and I was taken back as I had not seen him quite like this before.

YS: "I am being a bit sarcastic...yes we VARDAN Masters can at times, but know this. It's only because we are fed up with man's appalling disinterest and ignorance in the true spiritual life and how he clings to the illusions of this world."

"That is all for now. We will continue later on."

13

IMAGINATION AND PERFECTION
THROUGH ATTENTION

I have to say before I begin that, perfection is a great paradox. You may ask why, if I am the Living VARDAN Master, I don't know all things nor am I even remotely close to perfection on the outer. I was blessed to have Rebazar shed light upon much of this and this light will, perhaps, shed some profound realizations about your own true spiritual nature.

From the last discourse, I wondered a bit why Yaubl seems so excited and Rebazar Tarzs must have picked up on my thoughts as he often does. There is a communication between all beings who have an affinity for one another and this is especially true when we are dealing with kindred Souls who share the same ideals, although I am definitely the baby among these spiritual giants and often feel as if I am wearing diapers and they are humoring me to some degree.

Even though I have had many experiences deep in the heart of God and the upper worlds where few dwell, I am by no means putting myself on a pedestal. It seems the second we put ourselves above our fellow man, we are below him.

Oh no. It is only the degree of realization that each Soul has that sets them apart: the spiritual unfoldment and conscious awareness. This is why Paulji talked about VARDANKAR as the path of Total Awareness. We can only gain this through the spiritual exercises of VARDANKAR, but even then, only if we sincerely follow the path as laid down by the works and the Living VARDAN Master.

RT: "You were wondering about Yaubl?"

AF: "A little. You know I love him dearly as I love you."

RT: "You are learning much from being around him as I always do. You are finding that we ... Yaubl and I, among others are real people. Yes we are spiritual God beings for sure but we also have lower bodies, and have our own unique qualifications, and experiences and our own personalities, although they have long given in to the will of the HURAY, they are still present. They, as Yaubl has said before, are necessary."

AF: "Sometimes my personality and actions seem to go in contradiction with what is best for me."

Rebazar laughed.

RT: "Not now, we have other topics of a less personal and human nature to cover, mainly that of imagination and its use in these works known as VARDANKAR and formally known among many different names and disguises, including Eckankar under Paulji although, as you know Eckankar, while it exists in name is no longer the way back to God but, only a religion and not a particularly good one at that! But I digress."

"What is perfection?"

AF: "I do not know Master. But I do know it's found in the center of the HURAY."

RT: "Yes this is true. I cannot argue about what you have said but I will offer you more insight if I may."

AF: "Yes Master, please do."

RT: "Now bear with me here Allen for I am about to unlock a deep and dark mystery that once I unlock, it will seem far too obvious but, in this is, the key to all of the works. Where do we exist? I mean where are we?"

AF: "We are, here? I mean wherever we place our attention?"

RT: "Yes. Now where is perfection?"

AF: "Master I do not really know but I suppose it would be in the very center of the HURAY the Dhunatmik or that part of the HURAY that nothing can be said about whatsoever."

RT: "And there is also the Varnatmik, the outer visible and audible part of the HURAY that we can express; although words may be impossible this is the outer expression or outer side of the HURAY but, answer my question."

AF: "I am trying Master, but I take it I am off base?"

Rebazar began to laugh a jolly laugh.

RT: "The more you think and contemplate upon this, the stranger the question seems, does it not?"

"Do you see how ridiculous it is for the drop of God to try and answer? What is perfection?"

Rebazar laughed again.

"Man in his vanity has always tried to answer this question but it is insane to try, for no sooner than we think we have the answer; then we find it is not true! You see, thoughts and old experiences cannot take the place of reality no more than a photo can take the place of a loved one, or a picture of food can take the place of a meal!"

"We cannot own truth. We cannot buy truth; we can only experience truth and dwell in truth and become truth. But never do we reach, even remotely, perfection; only realization and the experience of God."

"Man talks about perfection and he talks about love, but he understands nothing!"

"What is love? I ask you now, what is love?"

AF: "It is the Audible Life Stream, the VARDAN in expression."

RT: "NO, it is not that at all. Love cannot be defined in mere words, nor can it be expressed in its totality. Love cannot be bottled up and sold nor truly understood. It must be lived but, this is not the answer either."

"What I am driving at is BEINGNESS! I AM THEREFORE I AM! The AMNESS of LIFE. The ISNESS of BEING and the BEINGNESS OF ISNESS. BEINGNESS! Say it out loud. NOW!"

AF: "BEINGNESS."

RT: "Now what is BEINGNESS? Define IT? Can you?"

AF: "No, I cannot."

RT: "Now we are getting somewhere. But where are we getting or, more accurately, what are we getting too? Do you even know?"

AF: "I feel as if I know nothing except for my meager experiences."

RT: "Do you even remember them? Do you even care? What precisely happened? You do not really know in the body do you? Do you?"

AF: "No. And yet I do."

RT: "Yes this is true. It's all true but none of it is true."

I looked at Rebazar and wondered; he had never been like this before. I knew he was trying to get a very important point across to me. So I waited.

RT: "Without BEINGNESS we have nothing. We are NOTHING! BEINGNESS cannot be defined. God cannot be defined. We speak of qualities. You speak of qualities but what qualities does God have? And why are they important?"

"Words are but man's feeble attempt to communicate. And yet why? What is the whole point of this? Why are you even here?"

"BEINGNESS!! Say it out load. Rejoice in its splendor for when you are in that holy of all holy places, you are in pure unadulterated BEINGNESS and the whole world could swirl around you like in some horrible storm, but it does not touch you in the least because you are in BEINGNESS! Dwelling in the Eternal Unchanging Consciousness and Total Awareness of God or HURAY ITSELF!"

"This is what man seeks. This is what you seek and yet you still do not understand. Hear you are the Living VARDAN Master and yet you don't completely understand this simple fact. That there is no place to go; there is nothing to do. But BE!"

"In BEINGNESS you have Eternity and in Eternity you have power, yes all the power you could ever want. All the Love, Wisdom and Freedom imaginable. More than you could ever use for you are now BEING in the center of the ALL. The true source of BEINGNESS is ISNESS and in ISNESS is BEINGNESS. This does not make sense to the mind. The mind cannot deal with this, so it tries to put everything into words and pretty pictures, and tie it all together with a big bow as if a Christmas present."

"The true Master does not need to utter a word for his BEINGNESS cannot be mistaken for anything else but the very presence of God ITSELF! Of HURAY."

"What is HURAY but BEINGNESS and ISNESS. I am that I am!"

"The ISNESS of BEINGNESS and the BEINGNESS OF ISNESS."

"There is one and only one way to understand me. And most will be lost in confusion and not understand."

"The only way is the way of BEINGNESS, and this is best accomplished on the path of VARDANKAR through the Margatma, the Living VARDAN Master and through the spiritual exercises and discourses laid down."

"Think about this. Some falsely believe that life is a process, or slow transformation or evolution, and that man evolves in consciousness and learns and grows."

"This is the way of the Kal Niranjan, king of the negative."

"If you are in a process and evolving, then you may not reach the end of such process. You may be in the middle, and what if you are in the middle; then what? Do you wait another 1000 lifetimes? Or a million lifetimes?"

"This is what the Kal wants everyone to believe. That life is a series of processes, much like some sort of industrial chemical plant where one reaction is followed by another, in a long chain of actions and chemical reactions that must all be done in a certain order and, over a period of time before the final product is delivered on the conveyor belt of life."

"This is the voice of the Kal speaking to man's astral and mental bodies. This is not truth nor is it the way to perfection in any way, shape or form."

"What man needs is an understanding of BEINGNESS and ISNESS!"

"If he develops his imaginative faculty; he has some hope of doing this ... but generally only with the assistance of the Living VARDAN Master can he find true answers to his questions."

"It is not the long list of questions that he needs answer to but one question. That of how to find, this BEINGESS and ISNESS of God, or HURAY."

"We must surrender to the Audible Life Stream and follow it into the worlds of BEINGNESS and ISNESS."

"Not the lower worlds where such things exist as shadows of

Truth, but in the higher worlds."

"First we find the perfect spiritual Master. Then we gain the secret initiations and receive the hidden instructions from the Ancient Masters as well as the Living VARDAN Master."

"Then we find through awareness, and consciousness and imagination, that beingness comes only through the control of our attention!"

"Ahh. Now you see. It is attention that offers us the key to Eternity; the key to BEINGNESS, ISNESS, to all things and places whether lower or higher."

"It, or attention has gotten us into this mess. The Kal has trained us to place our attention upon him. We worry, fear, lust after and live the Kal's plan for us; for the Kal has us in his grasp through imagination and attention."

"When we control our ability to place our attention through imagination and single-pointedness, we have a mighty key indeed."

"Now the principles of VARDANKAR, the Master, the Sound Current, the initiations and the spiritual exercises come into focus, for we have the missing piece of the puzzle."

"The control of attention."

"Once we do this, we are half way to God!"

"We must learn this single-pointedness and we place our attention eventually on God or the HURAY to such a point, that we surrender to IT and then the BEINGNESS overwhelms us, for we cannot tell where the HURAY begins and where we end and yet we, paradoxically, retain our individuality."

"What we are participating in is our expansion of consciousness. From that of the finite, to the less finite to the infinite. Of course, we never become God or the HURAY."

"We never obtain true perfection but we do enter into those secret and sacred worlds of BEINGNESS, and we may learn to carry this BEINGNESS with us for IT is now a part of us, if we will but let it. Then all beings who desire God are drawn up to us, for we possess the very consciousness of God through ITS BEINGESS and ISNESS."

"There is little that can be said about this subject other than, those who are ready will understand me on this and those who are not ready; it will make no sense to them."

"Before we reach this state, we must go through various lower levels of lesser Beingness and Isness. These are not the same as what I am speaking of here today but nevertheless, the same principles can be applied on a much lesser scale."

"Let us say we desire to receive the Beingness of a spiritual traveler who we desire to meet on the Astral Plane, say, in the Golden Wisdom Temple of Askleposis under Gopal Das."

"All things and beings have in their essence a form of Beingness therefore, we may to a lesser degree, find a being or place through this signature. It is almost like the zip code system at the U.S. post office. There is a signature and if we tune into a being or place's energy, we may be there at once!"

"Now Gopal Das has this signature, so does the actual Temple itself. These are all lesser states or forms of Beingness."

"If we are careful, we may find anyone or anything through this signature. It's simply a matter of placing our attention and imagination, and suddenly we are there."

"Once there, we can take in this lesser Beingness and Isness, and later if we desire to return to find this being or place, we need only use direct projection and we may go there immediately, for we are only placing our attention there and no more."

"We find, since time and space are an illusion, this is easy and we are really in all places at once but are, for the most part, unaware of this. Unless we are an accomplished Soul Traveler then we may be aware and if we are of the highest order or a VARDAN Master then we enter into the highest BEINGNESS and ISNESS imaginable that of the Margatma Consciousness and to a lesser degree that of the state of the Ocean of Love and Mercy."

"It is only at the Margatma state that we are with all beings in all places simultaneously, for in this state we are truly all present, all powerful and omniscient. As the VARDAN Masters say, Omnipresent, Omniscient; Omnipotent."

"This is only through the grace of the ISNESS of the HURAY that this is possible, for Soul truly is a drop from the Ocean of Love and Mercy but unlike a drop of water in an ocean, Soul can at this exalted level of consciousness be that which is ALL, and take on a part of the BEINGESS and ISNESS of the HURAY, and Universes upon Universes of the HURAY, as if this Soul is the HURAY and yet this Chosen Soul who takes on the Margatma Consciousness is clearly not the entire HURAY but yet contains this BEINGESS and ISNESS, therefore, is omnipresent, omnipotent and omniscient, and is able to be with all Souls and beings on every universe and every plane simultaneously."

"This should stagger the mind of man for I know it is hard for you to fully understand and you shall not until you more fully surrender to this BEINGNESS and ISNESS that I am speaking of here."

"Now you know some more of the secrets of the VARDAN adepts. We do not claim to know all things and yet our BEINGESS and ISNESS in God or HURAY does indeed, in a way, know all things and yet, of course, IT does not."

"We are a paradox as are you, don't you agree?"

AF: "Yes Master, this has been a most instructive discourse on BEINGNESS and ISNESS, but how does it apply to those who are not Masters but beginners on the path?"

RT: "Yes it does. For remember what I said about the nature of illusion and how the Kal wants us to believe in the slow method of processes and evolution?"

AF: "Yes Master."

RT: "So there you have it. Time and space being an illusion; those who are ready will understand and if they are wise place their feet solidly on the path of VARDANKAR and not look back. To look back is to invite the Kal into your consciousness. We must put our head forward and see the present moment within eternity and understand that the Master, that inner part of him, is taking care of us. This is your great responsibility to this world of putting the teachings out to the world and fulfilling your function as the Living VARDAN Master of the time."

"Those who judge you based on looks or personality, are not ready for they will not understand what you are saying."

"That is all for today. This topic is over but there is so much more to say. Soon over the next year or two, you will begin book three and four of the Shariyat-Ki-HURAY the Holy Book of VARDANKAR."

And with that Rebazar ended his fascinating talk and left me to ponder his exquisite words.

14

DOUBT AND ITS PLACE IN THE SPIRITUAL WORKS

RT: "Today I wish to speak upon the subject of doubt and its place in the spiritual works. Now I have often said, as all the VARDAN Masters say, that this world lay in the field of opposites. Good and bad, mountains and valleys, love and hate, etc; for everything, there is an opposite and this is the nature of the lower worlds of duality."

"We also have another factor in all of this: that of the inner vs. outer worlds of man, or the microcosm and the macrocosm."

"The third factor is one of belief. What we believe tends to become our overwhelming reality. And then there is faith, which ties into belief. When we have love, and belief and faith together, then our doubts begin to cease. This is neither good nor bad, but if we are going to find God and have selected the high path of VARDANKAR, then this is generally a good thing if we love the Master and have faith and belief in him."

"However strange this may sound to you, nothing is really necessary except a willingness to let go of all preconceived notions, dogma, superstition, cherished beliefs and ideals, and

119

simply be willing to test the Master's words through one's own efforts."

"In other words, if one is willing to let go of their preconceived opinions, and dogma and outdated belief systems or, at least temporarily suspend them, they can have the experience of God but only if they are willing to go out on a limb and be bold and adventurous."

"The mind, being negative in nature and made up of the Universal Mind Power, the father and mother of all minds, will throw up all manner of negative images but mostly doubt and the five passions or perversions of the mind."

"You see, doubt by itself is not bad; it is the unwillingness to let go of dogma and opinions and cherished beliefs and the five passions of the mind that is negative. It is lack of open-mindedness and lack of a willingness to experiment, be bold, adventurous and courageous. This is the disease that inflicts man. It is sheer laziness and nothing more."

"Man does not want to think. He does not want his world changed in any way that is uncomfortable to him. The real problem is lack of love; lack of love for God, lack of love for truth, lack of love for the Master and lack of compassion for his fellow man."

"If man truly loved himself and God, he would abandon his petty opinions and try with all his heart to follow the Master."

"He does not have to know for sure whether the Master is real; only be willing to let go and become detached and then put in the necessary effort."

"No true Spiritual Master cares whether the student believes him or not. The Master does not require that his chelas believe him; only that they suspend all judgment and try the techniques in order to prove them for themselves."

"If VARDANKAR was a religion, which it certainly is not, it would require things such as "Faith" and blind obedience."

"It certainly does not! In fact, VARDANKAR consists of many who are outside the box. Cliff-hangers, like Paul Twitchell, who represent a growing group of advanced Souls who are sick and tired of being told what to do, and worse, what to believe and feel; and now we have VARDANKAR which hopefully will be as free from dogma as possible."

"There will be many who will look at my words and say that VARDANKAR contains a certain amount of dogma. But they are failing to see the point. That VARDANKAR is not a religion, but the most complete path or science to Total Awareness and God Realization!"

"It's methodology is not original in the least, however, it is unique in that there is only one Living VARDAN Master at a time and it's best for the true truth seeker to accept this and study earnestly."

"It is natural to have doubts. This is the nature of life. Perhaps it is even a good thing. How many times does a Soul gets trapped because it accepts other people's postulates without much question?"

"The world is full of so called religions, and philosophical leaders, and gurus and teachers who will tell man that they and they alone know truth; and if the individual will just listen to them and have blind faith in all that they say, then all will be well in their lives."

"Some will accuse the Living VARDAN Master of

demanding faith and belief but this is not true. He only asks for a willingness and that those interested listen to him and make up their own minds. Frankly, as you know, he does not care either way whether someone believes him or not. He knows from experience that those who are ready will stay and experiment with the spiritual exercises and those that are not ready will find some excuse not to join him or even listen to what he has to say."

"This is fine. He does not need followers but only desires that those who truly desire God will listen to him in order to see whether VARDANKAR is something they desire to enter into as a beginning student."

"Then after a period of two years, they will know whether they desire their second initiation which will make them a true initiate upon the path."

"Until then, they are on a sort of probation period where they are able to evaluate whether the path is for them or not, and will study the Master's discourses which are designed to open them up spiritually and to teach Out-of-Body Tuza Travel so that they may consciously study at the various Golden Wisdom Temples of VARDAN with the Masters there and also partake of various experiences for their own spiritual growth."

"The problem most people face is they are not conscious of their travels into the various planes. They are not conscious of meeting with the Inner Master. They are unaware of what is going on and if they are not careful, they will discard VARDANKAR as being a false path with false teachers."

"What a lot of people fail to understand is that spiritual unfoldment takes time. That one cannot expect to go from nothing to the top of the world in a few weeks or months. Patience is a big factor and frankly it seems most chelas do not have enough patience to persevere through the dark nights of Soul and the times when nothing appears to be happening."

"But if the student will put in the effort, if he will engage in true contemplation upon the VARDAN works and read and re-read his nightly discourses, and practice his spiritual exercises daily for at least half an hour, he will make progress."

"But most are not even willing to do this. They would rather watch a TV movie than place their attention on Godly pursuits."

"There is no pursuit more Godly than VARDANKAR; for what could be better than transcending the human consciousness, transcending the psychic lower consciousness, moving past the astral, causal, mental and etheric planes and landing on the shores of the Ocean of Love and Mercy where dwells the HURAY, and where IT greets Soul and we take on our spiritual mission of being conscious co-workers with IT throughout all of eternity in any and all worlds that we chose to serve in!"

"Most do not believe such things are possible; or that if they are possible, they are fearful and push such things into the future."

"By pushing God and the God worlds out of the present moment and into some distant future, they are doing just that."

"What these people do not understand is that the future projected never comes. It is only in the here and now that God exists. If we are honest, we will realize that if we want to play games with God, we will not see the face of God."

"Yes, eventually, when our desire becomes such that we alter our priorities, we shall see the face of God, but this could be one thousand or one million lifetimes from now."

"If you don't pursue the high spiritual path of Out-of-Body Tuza Travel in this lifetime, what guarantee do you have that you will find God in the next? None!"

"Those who push God into the future say such trite things as "no one knows for sure" or "what is the rush ... we are all going to heaven eventually!"

"This is just laziness, but most who say these sorts of things are simply not ready. They do not understand that God is right here, right now and that they can have God only if they are willing to leave their physical bodies during contemplation and during the dream state, and go into those high, high, worlds or ecstatic states of consciousness that few men have ever known; but that the True Spiritual Travelers, the VARDAN Masters, can show them how to reach on a conscious and daily basis."

"What we are doing is becoming aware of that which already exists and has always existed throughout eternity. We are unfolding and learning to place our attention along certain states of awareness that are far finer in vibratory rate and far more alive than anything found in the lower worlds."

"This is not escapism for, in order to truly be a useful citizen of the universes upon universes of God, we must become aware. We must try and reach Total Awareness, Total Consciousness, Total Enlightenment, and the only way we can achieve this noble goal is through VARDANKAR and through Self and God Realization in the Pure Positive God Worlds."

"Nothing less will do and anything less is an illusion, although many times a mesmerizing illusion, if we make it into the Astral, Causal or Mental Plane and confront the rulers there or even partake of the vast stretches of beauty found in the lower worlds above the physical."

"It is true that even certain places on Earth are beautiful if that is all you are after. Certainly, places like Hawaii might qualify as a sort of lower world's paradise, so it's not hard to imagine that there are worlds upon worlds in the lower planes that are far more enchanting."

"If all we desire is enchantment, then we may stay in the lower worlds to suffer its slings and arrows. Its swing from positive to negative and back again upon the 'wheel of 84.'"

"This is what most Souls endure: lifetime after lifetime on the various lower worlds, spending time engaged in all manner of states of consciousness and activities ranging from positive to negative to neutral, over and over and over again almost ad infinitum."

"Some Souls have been at this for billions of years! In fact, many have done this and found, in the end upon graduation, that it was almost too easy to follow the Master out of these lower worlds into the shining worlds of light and sound, above the worlds of time and space."

"This is not to say the path of VARDANKAR is easy. Not in the least. Only that it is, in the long run, far easier then enduring thousands or even millions of past lives that seem to never end."

"The lost Souls are not really lost, or at least it's only temporary, for eventually they will find their way. But the way of the Kal through perfection of the personality and lower bodies is not the way of God. It is the slow way and not direct at all."

"It is the way of pain and suffering. Although at times, of

course, there will be pleasure; it is a worldly pleasure consisting of varied experiences of emotions, physicality, thoughts, ideals and feelings too vague to be totally real and, yet, too mesmerizing to be easily ignored."

"If all one wants is a life of experiences in the lower worlds of time and space, then certainly that is common and ordinary."

"There is no real action required, nor real effort. The lords of karma will take care to see that a Soul gets plenty of experience on the Physical and Astral regions, mostly the physical worlds and various planets."

"If this is all a person desires, then they need read no further for they are on the path of death and rebirth and can simply take up some conventional religious teaching or philosophy."

"Most of the good ones only talk about karma: that what you sow you reap. This is true. And it is certainly wise not to increase our karmic burden by violating other's psychic space by, say, murdering their physical body, or stealing their wife or gold."

"But if one thinks this is all there is to the spiritual life; then they are sadly missing the point of all cosmic existence!"

"The path of righteousness is the path of pain and suffering. Even if one were as careful as possible to not injure another person, which is virtually impossible given their lower state of spiritual awareness, they still are not going to find God, nor truth."

"Being "Good" is like being an Actor on a stage giving a performance. No matter how well they perform, they are still in an artificial and severely limited environment."

"In order to enter into the VARDAN stream or spiritual

stream of life, also known as the Audible Life Stream, one must submerge themselves into it freely and willingly."

"In order to do this, one needs the Master in order to act as a sort of spiritual bridge and way shower, and guide us past the rocks and shoals of life into the splendid worlds of light and sound above the etheric worlds."

"Then one needs the initiation which links one directly with the various planes, the spiritual exercises and, of course, they need the HURAY. There is little else in life that is important than these four things."

"There will be times when we may doubt our own divinity; we may doubt God or ourselves. We may doubt the Master. We may even doubt our own spiritual perceptions and past experiences on the inner planes. Some even find themselves doubting their sanity."

"Doubt is simply part of the testing that is required in order to reach the higher worlds and establish oneself there in full consciousness. It is not the doubt that we must fear but our own fear and the paralyzing effects that it can create in our spiritual life. Fear and doubt are two things that can destroy one if combined together."

"But if we have doubt without fear, then we can move forward and confront matters. We can continue on with our spiritual exercises and true contemplation upon the spiritual works. We can venture out of our bodies and do various creative experiments and test the Master's words every step of the way."

"If we combine fear with doubt, we have a bitter form of paralysis that is far worse than cancer."

"Fear and doubt create the inability to move. To venture outward or inward. This is what the Kal or king of the negative power desires: that we have both fear and doubt together. Then we can become trapped inside our own skulls and bodies and are finished spiritually if we can't overcome this deadly combination."

"The VARDAN Masters teach detachment or VAIRAG. When we are detached, then we can face doubt head on and try the various methods outlined in the discourses and outer works, as well as beginning to be conscious and partake more of the inner works which occur in the various Golden Wisdom Temples and throughout our day, especially during our spiritual exercises and at night while we sleep."

"No true VARDAN Master will interfere with another's state of consciousness without their permission. This is a direct violation of spiritual law and must never be done."

"Therefore, one has to be careful about their own personal belief systems. This is one very important reason why the VARDAN Masters caution those considering the path to let go or drop all dogma, superstitions, cherished beliefs and opinions. We find that VARDANKAR flies in the face of all conventional so-called wisdom. It certainly flies in the face of religion, metaphysics and philosophy and most if not all of the teachings out there … for the true VARDANist does not worship the Kal power or the Universal Mind Power. His goal is not cosmic consciousness or universal love."

"These are things of the Mental Plane and lower and are not real. They are the false teachings of false masters and, if anyone wants to follow this sort of thing, that is their business and the VARDAN Masters will not interfere. They will simply withdraw their presence and let the individual decide his own path. They do this even while knowing that it may be hundreds, thousands or even millions of lifetimes before they are ready."

"All Souls must choose their own way. But the HURAY does, in some instances, bring a ready Soul to the path but, even when this happens, that Soul can refuse and the Master will do nothing and allow this to happen, knowing full well what is happening but not be able to speak of it."

"It is a fact that the Master knows many things he cannot talk about. You, as a new Master, are learning this but it will get to the point where you will know all and yet not be able to speak of any of it and must wait patiently for those Souls to do as they please. Often, you will not say a word. I know this has happened to you before ... and sometimes you did say something and over stepped your bounds a few times. But you are learning the law of non-interference which is tied in with the law of love that supersedes all other laws."

"Getting back to one of my main points here; because these lower worlds contain opposites, there will always be doubt. We are dealing with attention and states of BEINGNESS. When we enter into a state of BEINGESS then there is no doubt, but when we leave this state there is doubt. We must basically ignore the child-like mind as it cries and whines."

"Those who are worried about doubt often are too involved with their minds and identify strongly with all of their thoughts and opinions, and mental and emotional impressions."

"This becomes their entire world and they don't know of any other. We must relax and realize that the mind is like an unruly child. What would a loving mother do if her 4 year old child was throwing a tantrum on the middle of a highway while traveling 60 miles per hour? If the child demanded that she stop the car in the middle of the highway, would she comply? Of course not! She would not follow the directions of this child but take charge of the road ahead. She might pull into a rest stop later on, but she certainly is not going to let her 4 year old direct her driving. This would be dangerous to say the least."

"And yet, as ridiculous as this idea of a 4 year old child telling an adult to stop in the middle of a busy highway, most people will listen to their mind and be compelled to do whatever it says, even if IT's to their spiritual detriment."

"We must, through Out-of-Body Tuza Travel, learn to leave our bodies so that we may partake of the divine Love, Wisdom, Power and Freedom that exists outside of the human state of awareness. Then we shall know all things but only if we are wise and not let our mental and emotional bodies rule our world, but instead treat them as servants instead of our masters."

AF: "Master, how does one control his mind and passions of the mind?"

RT: "The mind runs in grooves. It is almost like a railroad track except it's far harder to change. With a railroad track, you can pull up the rails and relay them in another direction."

"It is far easier to bend steal than change the mind. With steal you can use force. You can use heat and hammers and other equipment to bend steal to your specifications. With the mind, it is not so easy."

"This is another topic and we will … if you desire it … cover in another discourse. You are tired and it is time to eat and rest my dearest one. You are doing well. You're managing to write more and this is important. I want to say before we close this discourse; on another note that if one is willing to go out on a limb, they can gain amazing spiritual progress.

What I mean by this is, when one does things they do not

feel are possible such as writing about VARDANKAR or giving a talk, and anything that they feel is beyond their mortal abilities and they attempt it with all their hearts despite their feelings of inadequacy, they are bound to find something extraordinary. What they will soon discover, if they are brave and adventurous, is that the VARDAN will step in and use them and all of a sudden they are producing works and doing works that they are not capable of."

"For example, one may not feel they are ready to give a talk. Let's say they are asked by the Master to give a half hour talk on a topic pertaining to VARDANKAR such as Reincarnation. And, let us say, they do not feel worthy or able to give such a talk but they push these doubts aside and put in the necessary effort."

"Their mind may be blank at the start, but if they surrender to the VARDAN and Inner Master, if they declare themselves a vehicle for the HURAY, Margatma and VARDAN, then surrender and let spirit or the VARDAN take over, an amazing thing will happen. They will discover that spirit is using them in ways they could not even imagine."

"But I have to add that we need to develop our abilities and read, study, contemplate, etc. so that when spirit tries to use us, we are ready as best we can be ready. But basically, it's about surrender and detachment and not about great intellectual and emotional powers, nor about being a charismatic speaker or eloquent writer, but about doing our spiritual exercises and then out-flowing spirit or the VARDAN into this dark world for those Souls who clamor for truth."

"That is all for now."

15

THE FIVE PASSIONS OF THE MIND: PART 1

RT: "Today I am going to speak of the five passions or perversions of the mind and go into some greater details as well as talk about Lady Maya, the word Maya meaning illusion."

"There is a story that there is this goddess some call Lady Maya. She speaks to men through their hearts, minds, body and emotions and whispers sweet nothings into their ear. She promises whatever it is that is of their fondest desire but her true purpose is to prevent Soul from Tuza Travel."

"For every man and woman, her whispers will vary. For some, it will be religion and dogma that traps them, for others, materiality and love for a material space God who promises them heaven and the things and of this world. For most, it will be a combination of many things."

"Most men falsely believe that they can easily outwit her but her secret is that she knows the hearts of all men and can find any weaknesses and exploit them with ease."

"There is only one cure. One way of overcoming her in the end and that is the way of VARDANKAR, in particular of placing one's attention upon the Master and the Audible Life Stream."

"We must declare ourselves channels of the Master,

VARDAN and HURAY and do all in ITS name. We must become humble before the Master and not get cocky or too self-assured. At the same time, we must not bring false humility upon ourselves and grovel in the mud and dirt and feel guilt, or false humility that we are somehow inferior and will never make it to God."

"Her dreams, that is Lady Maya, are so luring and compelling that few can overcome them without the Master and utter and total reliance upon him and God."

"We must chant the holy names constantly. An idle mind and hands are the devil's workshop, or so the saying goes."

"We find that if we are not serving the VARDAN, we are serving the Kal. We must serve something. We must choose a consciousness to channel into this world and all the other worlds and so if we fail to choose or pick sides, the automatic human tendency is to serve the Kal as its channel."

"The five passions of the mind, once again, are Lust, Anger, Greed, Attachment and Vanity."

"Entire volumes could be written about these passions and their almost countless brothers and sisters."

"Man, for the most part, serves the Kal or lower forces and does not even recognize it! Whenever one tries to make this world a better place instead of finding Spiritual Liberation, what they are saying is that this world is man's home, and he should dwell here and not go back to God. This is the way of the Kal."

"Whenever a man engages in violence, murder, robbery and the hurting of innocent people, he is a channel of the Kal, but also whenever one engages in the avid practice of pompous religious ceremony, meaningless gestures designed to strike emotional chords, the emotional elation of feeling special and accomplished, accolades and awards, or any of a trillion exercises that have little or nothing to do with God, again they are engaged in the Kal consciousness."

"Whether they create good karma or bad karma will, of course, depend on a number of factors but the point is that whatever delays man's journey back to God is of the Kal or negative, and whatever facilitates that journey is of the positive or VARDAN stream of consciousness."

"Man will find no peace in this world. He will seek comfort in the things of this world. In the riches of wealth, the house of power, the house of love, the house of knowledge and many other places. He will go to the four corners of the Earth and beyond seeking love, happiness, sex, drugs, honor, admiration, wisdom, power and freedom, but he will find none of these things here unless he meets up with the Living VARDAN Master or one of his true disciples and places himself firmly on the path of VARDAKAR."

"Why is this so? It is a bit obvious but God cannot be found in the Kal. It is not the nature of the Kal nor his lower world kingdom to be the true home of Soul, for the mighty HURAY dwells in ITS humble abode in the Ocean of Love and Mercy and has little concern for these lower worlds. They are nothing more than schools to teach Souls to return back to God after they have received an education."

"Those who cling to conventional wisdom, to science, religion, politics, social reform, philosophy, metaphysics, dogma and superstition will only find pain."

"Those who are steeped in the worlds of Kal and his ways will fight those who preach the path of VARDANKAR, or the path of Total Awareness through Out-of-Body Tuza or Soul

Travel. There is always fighting between these two systems, for VARDANKAR has always been a threat to the Kal power and the Kal will defend his dominance and enslavement over those Souls that he controls through Lady Maya and his ways and methods of enslavement."

"Lady Maya will make one believe they are a world savior, or that they are here to save the planet, or that the object or objects of their affection or attention are more important than God ITSELF!"

"She will put dreams into the hearts and minds of the unsuspecting and make them her slaves for as long as possible."

"Look around you! What do you see?"

"Most men live in a pathetic zombie-like state of hypnotic suggestion from the Kal and his channels."

"Talk to most people and you will see all sorts of strange states of consciousness. Most men are so busy trying to get ahead in this world or trying to survive that God plays little or no part in their lives. They have no time for God; only for their own survival, or worse, their own selfish goals and aspirations, that when analyzed, mean nothing and are generally based either on the five passions of the mind or on the idea that this world is to be made into a heaven on Earth."

"This world will never be Soul's true home. It will never be a heaven but the Kal desires everyone to believe this lie! It desires man to remain here for as long as possible and not leave the body or, if man does leave the body, to venture in the lower to mid Astral regions where the Kal reigns supreme in his own domain!"

"Lady Maya will work with each Soul to try and stop it from reaching perfection. Many fail to be worthy of finding the

Master and of those who do; few appreciate what he is offering and complain that the teachings are not free or that they are not designed to manifest wealth, happiness, sex and material success here on Earth."

"He will declare, either secretly to himself or even publicly, that VARDANKAR has nothing to offer anyone. That it is a fraud and that there is no value in it whatsoever. He will go on to attack it or ignore it, for man generally seeks the comforts of this world and will listen to anyone who promises him some sort of physical, emotional or mental improvement in his condition in life. He desires health, wealth, sex, human love, the admiration of his fellow man, personality worship if at all possible and the good will of all men towards him. He desires to be liked and even loved by as many as possible. Worshiped and looked up to and generally living in a lifestyle that places him above his fellow man and yet allows him to exploit human beings for sex, friendship, companionship, material gain, labor and time, ego gratification etc, etc, etc."

"Most men will never admit these deep dark desires but, nevertheless, they have them lurking around inside their subconscious or even conscious mind. There is little space left for God; for materiality has taken up most if not all of their attention and, frankly, they have no plans of changing this and, in fact, will kill in order to maintain their own limited state of sleeplike consciousness and materiality."

"Frankly, the idealists are little better. They desire many of the same things. Only it is sugar coated as in being good for humanity as a whole. They still desire health, wealth, sex, admiration, friendship, power, etc; they just desire a different flavor of such things."

"They may do volunteer work or work towards some noble cause of feeding the homeless or helping abandoned orphans.

While this is certainly an improvement and will most likely create some good karma, this will still keep them trapped in the lower worlds; for the only way to find God is through Out-of-Body Tuza Travel and not through physical, emotional and mental activities."

"One can dance, sing, read, write, play the piano, shout, give lectures, win friends and influence people. Paint pictures and build monuments. One can be kind, loving, compassionate, studious, unselfish, insightful, scholarly, helpful, dedicated to helping others and the list goes on."

"But all any of this can do is create good karma, never bring one to God."

"It is like the fool who jumps on top of the car in a frantic attempt to start the motor vehicle."

"He can jump onto of the hood all he wants but until he inserts the key into the ignition and turns it, the car will not start nor will he go anywhere in it."

"Man can try and please God but none of his activities actually touch the hem of God nor bring him closer to God in any meaningful way. They act as distractions. They are in effect counterfeit spirituality."

"It is good to do good works but not at the expense of failing to return into those high, high, Pure Positive God Worlds and consciously dwelling within them."

"The goal of helping ones fellow man is a negative goal. Although this flies in the face of the orthodox thinking, I am prepared to stand behind this statement."

"We must, instead, serve God consciously by learning to

dwell consciously in the higher worlds and become aware."

"We can only reach this Total Awareness and Self and God Realization through the spiritual exercises of VARDANKAR and through the methods outlined by the VARDAN Masters in the books, discourses and lectures. There is no other way and the sooner we realize this, the faster we can find truth and return to God and become a useful spiritual citizen; a conscious co-worker with the HURAY throughout all eternity."

"The five passions have a twofold negative effect.
1. They distract us from the high path and from God.
2. They suck us into the possibility of creating all manner of karma through the breaking of spiritual law."

"The first of these is bad enough but combined with the second, we have a deadly combination to contend with."

"The first is probably the most insidious for Soul exists in the present moment, therefore, if the Kal power or Lady Maya can distract us and keep our attention off of Self and God Realization, we are in trouble."

"Do not fear Lady Maya or the Kal for we have some powerful methods that have been perfected since time immortal. This is not to say it will be easy. The tests will be overwhelming at times but we can make things easier if we follow some general principles."

"First, we must have total sincerity in our desire to find God! This must be unwavering and we must be free of all dogma and personal attachments to opinions."

"Second, we need to achieve the one-pointed consciousness. We must learn clever ways of not only focusing on God but of being single-pointed in our desire and attention. We must learn to keep our focus on what is important to us; namely, the Inner Master, the VARDAN and the HURAY."

"Equally important, we must learn to divert our attention away from the Kal and Lady Maya. Since this is a tricky thing, we can place the image of the Living VARDAN Master upon the screen of the Tisra Til or third eye located about one inch between the eye brows.

"The Inner Master, who is the personalization of the HURAY and VARDAN, then acts as a sort of guardian and filter to keep all that is streaming in, or that consciousness that is streaming in and the consciousness that is streaming out or out-flowing from us pure and of the VARDAN."

"When we do pick up negative Kal impressions, we must not let them disturb us but simply watch them as if we are sitting on a placid river watching barges gently float by us from a distance."

"The mind is composed mostly of the Kal so we need not panic or get upset; we simply recognize that there is no need to judge ourselves based upon our lower bodies; based upon our thoughts or feelings. Nor should we be overly critical about our actions and words."

"If we make a mistake and say or do the wrong thing, we simply need to recognize that in the lower bodies we are not perfect."

"But as Soul, our eternal God self, we are perfect; we only lack in the realization of that perfection but can obtain such realization through VARDANKAR and the Master."

"Attention is the spiritual coin that opens many doors. But again, this attention must be free of dogma, cherished beliefs and opinions. We must become born anew and let go of the old states of consciousness. One cannot let the VARDAN and Master in if he desires to pick and choose."

"Frankly, this is one of the greatest problems the Master faces. The students or would-be students want to pick and choose what they are willing and not willing to do and believe. It is like the man who comes to learn piano from the master Musician but then declares that he is not willing to practice more than 10 minutes a day and that he will not do his exercises but only wants to play jazz and will not use his pinkies when playing and does not want to use the pedals at all and only play a grand piano that is white with a beige stripe."

"Such an individual will most likely never become an accomplished Pianist for he is so engrossed in picking and choosing, that he prevents his own progress and makes it virtually impossible for the Master to teach him anything."

"The VARDAN Masters do not ask their new chelas to believe everything they are told but to remain open-minded and prove it for themselves. This is the ideal situation, for the Master will give many instructions for clever ways of leaving one's body and Tuza Traveling into the various worlds and meeting the various VARDAN Masters in the Golden Wisdom Temples of VARDAN.

"The first thing that most need to learn is that their training on other paths, besides VARDANKAR, does not really qualify them and is not of much use. In other words, if someone studied another path for 15 or 20 years most, if not all of what they learned, will be of little use to them now."

"They have to move on and let go of the past and realize that most, if not all of what they know, is wrong and contrary to truth. This is a humbling experience indeed but it is necessary and the faster we recognize this fact, the faster we will move into the conscious awareness of the higher worlds. So it is a blessing for those willing to let go of their vanity long enough to see they are the most fortunate or fortunate for being on the most direct path back to the HURAY: VARDANKAR."

"I have digressed a bit but had to in order to cover some important points. We shall rest then, I will get back to the topic of the five passions or perversions of the mind and how they delay Soul to returning to God and how to overcome them.

16

THE FIVE PASSIONS OF THE MIND: PART 2

RT: "This topic could be written about in several volumes and not even scratch the surface so what I need to do is give you an overview, but mostly focus on answers rather than the problem. Still, we must cover all bases as best we can, given the space and time limitations.

"Part of the problem is that the ego self or lower self does not understand what is happening because it, of itself, is sunk in illusion and Maya. You see, the lower self is of the Kal or universal mind power and being of this, Kal cannot be conscious of anything.

"It is only Soul who has awareness or consciousness. This is the secret for all of life! Remember it well. The mind cannot know anything. It is Soul. Now Soul, working through a mind, may know certain things but the mind acts as a sort of barrier or filter and as a filter, it strains out much good. That is, the mind is more like a filter in reverse where it filters out much good or the pure positive VARDAN and allows or mixes what gets through with Maya.

"Maya is really the VARDAN or Universal Sound Current in expression at a much lower level of beingness. When the

VARDAN mixes with matter, energy, time and space, it becomes much more dense and Soul becomes frantic to find truth because it finds itself painfully aware that it is not home but in enemy territory. The mind or ego self has 4 functions.

"They are: Chitta, Manas, Buddhi and Ahankar.

"Chitta, becomes aware of form, beauty, color, rhythm, harmony, and perspective. Enjoys these things and rejects what it doesn't like."

"Manas, known as mind stuff. Receives and registers impressions through the senses of smell, taste, hearing and feeling. Chief function is taste. Enjoys or rejects whatever it does not like."

"Buddhi, discrimination and decision. Intellect. It is the channel that Soul uses as Its chief instrument of thought and when endowed by the VARDAN it produces thought. It cannot function unless it is empowered by the VARDAN."

"Ahankar, accepts the decisions of the other faculties handed on to it by the Buddhi. Makes the I-ness of the individual."

"Now the Ahankar is the main faculty of the mind that needs to be discussed here today! But the others of course are also important. Ahankar makes up the individual I-ness. Now this is essential and nether bad nor good but is simply a necessary part of living in these lower worlds of M.E.S.T."

"Now the two points I want to make are deceptively simple."

"Number one: When exaggerated Ahankar becomes Egotism or Vanity. Now I am speaking here today of an undue exaggeration where it turns into one of the most deadly of the five passions of the mind."

"Point number two is this….that Ahankar is that faculty that helps the individual "I" distinguish itself from others. Now Soul uses this Ahankar in Its spiritual growth in these lower worlds. Being that it differentiates one Soul from another Soul we can hardly exist in the lower worlds without this faculty intact and active. However there is a great struggle that takes place as the VARDAN and Kal fight over who or what gets to use the individual "I" consciousness. This struggle can be quite painful see…and this is the great battle that most face if not all face in their quest to find Spiritual Mastership in a single lifetime. It is never easy although for some it is easier than for others, but the VARDAN will demand more and more of the individual until it has all of him! Do you understand this?"

A.F. "Yes Master, I think so."

RT. "Then we have an understanding here, that this great struggle for the individual cannot be altered nor shirked. We cannot get absorbed into the universe as many Far Eastern paths teach. This is entirely wrong! See? What we must do is recognize that the HURAY or God is in fact only interested in the individual. If it was interested in the group this would not make sense for the group consists of only individual Souls. A group of Souls does not move together like some flock of sheep being herded. This is the religious ideal that man has in order to maintain his herd instinct and try and feel safe and avoid thinking or self-responsibility. Finally by the time one finds VARDANKAR the Ancient Science of Tuza or Soul Travel they must recognize that the individual is always more important than the group. It is the individual that finds Self Realization and it is the individual that finds God Realization and eventually VARDAN Mastership. Never the group. There is no exception to this rule! None what so ever! Do I make myself clear here?"

A.F. "Yes. I know this is a sore point for many in the new age movement who speak about Ascension and also for those who meditate and try and bliss out or reach enlightenment through passivity and the Cosmic Consciousness state."

R.T. "Correct! This has nothing to do with true Self Realization let alone God Realization and is definitely not the goal of VARDANKAR in the slightest, but only a beginning step on the path."

"But please remember this. That things are not what they appear to be and many who feel they are highly developed spiritually are NOT and many who think they are not highly developed spiritually in fact are very advanced. Things are not as they appear to many. The HURAY or God does not judge us based on the same criteria as man and the Human state of consciousness! So there is often more hope spiritually for the wino laying out in the gutter than for the priest or do-gooder who thinks he or she is a selfless example of pious goodness!"

Rebazar had a smile upon his face that did not seem to go away as he continued on.

R.T. "There is generally much suffering in the beginning as the Chela or want to be chela faces himself and this struggle can seem dark and almost ominous as the two faces, that of the Kal and that of the VARDAN fight for the control of Ahankar as well as the other 3 faculties of the mind of man! It is really quite dramatic at times to view this struggle and it can reach almost cosmic epic proportions in the microcosmic universe of the individual who is engaged in this struggle!"

"All spiritual growth must come through the opening and development of these faculties; mainly through the Ahankar, the executive faculty of the mind."

"When spiritual training is started as I stated, generally there is this period of suffering and hardships. This is due to the retraining of the Ahankar, the executive faculty, and the other three functions of the mind."

"Now the mind is a complex machine and has nothing except when animated by the VARDAN or spirit of God. The mind is much like a gigantic motor or computer that cannot exist without electrical power to run or animate it! Without the VARDAN mind is dead and lifeless."

"One need not be concerned with the mind or identify with mind for it is not our true self but only a glorified machine that only appears to have enormous power when animated by Spirit. None the less Spirit must use mind while in these lower worlds and so must Soul! Therefore this great suffering appears quite real to the individual when he or she is in the throes of struggle! It is a great test. How strong is the Soul and is its love for the HURAY and truth greater than its petty attachments to the mind stuff and the things of this world?"

"Most will fail these long periods of testing for they are not yet worthy of God!"

"The Masters generally will stand by waiting for they usually will not interfere. This is a time of great testing and it can happen at any time not just during the beginning of their spiritual training. Sometimes they will literally shake in their boots so to speak and suffer greatly. This internal struggle can go on for days, weeks, months or even years. If they refuse to surrender or do not love God or the True Spiritual Traveler enough to surrender then the struggle may carry into a future lifetime. The Master will generally do nothing for this is a test and if the Master were to interfere it may ruin everything. This is a little known fact. That those who struggle must face their own worst fears and look deep into the mirror. God has no time nor patience for those who are too afraid of their own reflection in the mirror to take a good cold hard look at themselves. Those who hate or fear themselves in turn hate or fear God ITSELF. And God has no time for this. How can one face God if they refuse to face themselves? They cannot!!! It's impossible!!!"

"The mind is of a negative nature of course, so Soul and the VARDAN must maintain control at all times otherwise we become channels for the Kal power and then wonder why we appear to have failed on the spiritual path. It is not that there is anything wrong with Soul our true Eternal Self other than the fact that we have become lazy and let the mind run on automatic pilot and the Kal power has taken over. Much like falling asleep at the wheel of an automobile."

"We will pick up again after we have rested."

* * * * *

R.T. "Picking up where we left off on the subject of mind and the control of one's focus or attention, one could say that man's life consists of almost infinite moments within eternity of almost infinite choices to decide whether he wants to participate in the higher states of consciousness or wallow in the irrelevant sea of the Kal or negative consciousness."

"When will man stop thinking that he can delay his journey to God without consequences? When we choose to forgo the VARDAN and pass on these infinite opportunities to find God in this moment, we lose ourselves in irrelevant experiences of becoming that for which we are not ... or the unreal. If man wants to wallow in the Kal or unreal, that is his decision but the foolishness comes from the fact that man does not even know he is making a choice, but thinks he is simply drifting in a sea of irrelevant moments within time and space ... instead of missing the boat spiritually by not taking hold of the Master's hand and grasping the Audible Sound Current of VARDAN and riding it back into full awareness of eternity and the true pure ecstatic God worlds beyond time and space. The purpose of the Kal is to delay this journey for as long as possible and so Lady Maya whispers sweet nothings into the ear of man, blinding him to the light and making him deaf to the Audible Life Stream or VARDAN; so he fails to realize the sanctity of each and every moment.

"Every moment is an opportunity found within eternity to experience the God Worlds and the worlds of Seeing, Knowing and pure Beingness or an opportunity to wallow in the worlds of illusion and stay in the confines of these lower worlds. This battle or choice exists in every moment of eternity and man in the worlds of time and space thinks these choices represent moments in time and thinks they are nothing. That he can just go from irrelevant moment to irrelevant moment and choose Lady Maya as if her dreams are his.

"This is the nature of the Kal and Kali or male and female aspects of the Kal Niranjan, king of the negative.

"That of death and the lower aspects of man and reincarnation and the deterioration of what is good, born of the positive and negative energies of life. The alternating fields of opposites joined by the neutral power."

"If one wants to follow the Kal or negative power and the universal mind power, that is their choice but it is a sickness and the five passions of the mind is the disease.

"When one is sick, he must seek help or die. When one is sick with the disease of the Kal: that of countless incarnations within the lower worlds of pain and pleasure, one must seek a cure if they are wise. This cure to countless incarnations is VARDANKAR but man, in his ignorance, frowns on this and Lady Maya whispers that her sweet nothings are the essence of life itself and that life is nothing but these endless moments within time and space.

"She and the Kal promise nothing but happiness in the hereafter but it never comes in the long run, because Soul is not of this world and can never find fulfillment in the Kal or worlds of illusion; only in the VARDAN and in Self and God Realization far above the Kal worlds of illusion, beyond time, space, matter and energy."

"Man is dark and will try and destroy anything outside of his illusions so the VARDAN Masters generally go into hiding; for many a time they have been driven into oblivion by the powers of Kal who seeks to destroy them."

"It is rare that they may go public, therefore, when they do, it is very wise to seek them out and take up the path, otherwise only a very small band may find them when they are in hiding in this world due to the attacks upon them from the Kal."

"No matter what they do, they are attacked; but when the political climate is somewhat tolerant of freedom, they at times will go public at their own risk in order to give more Souls the outer opportunity to find the path back to God."

"The Kal and its channels will try and stop them as they did with Paul Twitchell, who was poisoned in Spain and his work, hounded by the likes of mediocre minds who failed to understand him and attacked him, not realizing who or what he was."

"This will happen to you too if you are not careful and therefore, you must be careful of those Kal channels who lurk like dark shadows in the night trying to destroy the children and father of the light; for they will claim they are of the light but be not deceived for darkness falls upon this Earth every time they show their ugly faces."

"They try and destroy God's true channels, therefore they hate God and hate life ITSELF and love the Kal and death, pain, rebirth and suffering upon the 'wheel of 84.' They are delusionary, although they accuse the Margatma of being delusional for they of themselves have no ears to hear nor eyes to see truth; so they project their negative consciousness wherever they go through clever words of darkness and appalling ignorance of truth and light."

"The ego of man gives him nothing but trouble. While it is necessary to have an ego and lower bodies while living in these lower worlds, I cannot emphasize enough the danger of the ego or little self and the danger of the mind taking charge of Spirit or more accurately, trying to control spirit and the life of the individual. When the mind of man attempts to control spirit instead of the other way around, there is nothing but pain, death, destruction and rebirth in an endless cycle of karma or cause and effect. Man cannot break free until he learns to let go of karma and love God more than his little self and puny mind."

"The universal mind power which, like I said earlier, is the father and mother of all minds, appears great to man. He thinks it contains the sum total of all Love, Wisdom and Power but he is mistaken. Only the HURAY is real and man will not find rest inside of the universal mind power. He may find a temporary dwelling place in the astral, causal or mental planes, where time appears to exist in a less linear state and it appears that the

150

beings living there are eternal in nature. But this is simply not true. If a being lives for, say, 10,000 Earth years, is this eternal in nature or is it temporal?"

"I say unto you this, we must become very familiar with these five passions or perversions of the mind and know them like the backs of our hands, if we are to find peace in these lower worlds."

"But most of all, we need to place our attention solemnly upon the HURAY and Living VARDAN Master and stop this senseless fighting with the Master and God over pointless points.
Instead of arguing with the Master or rejecting the Master, man should be listening with intensity to what the Master has to say and trying to understand him."

"This is seldom the case. Man will listen to stories of how to improve his material place in this world, how to find human love, devotion, money, health and material happiness. Man will listen and listen and pay his hard earned money for advice and books; even join groups on how to manifest the material life."

"But mention to him of Tuza or Soul Travel and returning to the Pure Positive God Worlds and most men yawn, or worse, become angry and want to kill the messenger."

"Man cannot tolerate truth and must have lies and illusion, otherwise he becomes very uncomfortable."

"This is one very important reason why the path of VARDANKAR is almost always cloaked in secrecy or underground. Man wants the things of the Kal or Kal power in his life much more then he desires the HURAY."

"The God of most men is a god that lets him have what he

wants. Mainly, defeating his enemies, gives him emotional peace, sex, human love, a loving mate, money, the admiration of his friends and family and entire community, power and the things of this world and lastly, an emotional elation and happiness or feeling of happiness. It matters little to most men why they are happy. Only that they feel an emotional feeling of happiness. It could be caused by something as mundane as sexual gratification or even winning a tennis match and proving his superiority over other men."

"Yes, man is an ego creature and until he tames his ego, he will not find peace nor God. He must become clever and learn Out of Body Tuza Travel with the Master otherwise he wallows in the lower planes, mostly the Astral and Physical planes where he is a prisoner of his own ignorance and the Kal Niranjan."

"Man is all puffed up with self-importance! This is vanity at its worst. Man is never happy but always seeking answers from outside himself; never once listening to the still voice within and surrendering to God with total sincerity."

"One cannot pick and choose when attempting to return to the Great HURAY. One must surrender and let go of all that stands between him and God. To do otherwise, is simply courting disaster and or failure. Often both and rather quickly, I may add."

"But the VARDAN Masters do not force themselves upon man. They let man make his own mistakes and let him learn his own lessons, even if those lessons may divert his attention from God for a million or a billion lifetimes; they will generally do little or nothing until the individual invites them into his or her consciousness. Then the Masters will help any and all who are sincere in desiring to find God."

"But woe to he who is the pretender and only says he desires

God, for he is the false prophet. One cannot play games with God. One may fool their fellow man but not God, nor the Great Spirit or Audible Life Stream known as the VARDAN."

"You cannot hide anything from the VARDAN nor God; only from yourself and your fellow man. But even this does not work in the long run: the lower worlds reek of insincerity and lies."

"It is a shadow of a shadow, of a shadow of a reflection of truth."

"The five passions are the mortar that holds the karmic bricks into place and cements man's entrapment in the lower worlds of time and space. Only through the Law of Love, which supersedes all other laws, can man escape. But this only works if he is willing to accept the Margatma, the Living VARDAN Master and surrender without holding onto his past feelings, opinions, beliefs and dogma."

"If a man says he desires God but is unwilling to surrender all to God, then he does not desire God enough to find God. He is only a fool."

"It is said, as you have heard countless times, that when we give the Master all that we possess, the Master, in turns, gives us all that he possesses. We do not have to give up our family, our home, our job or our material wealth. What I am speaking of here is giving up the last vestiges of the ego and surrendering our inner self or spiritual side to the Inner Master, to the VARDAN and to the HURAY."

"It does not matter what we have done in the past. All past karma can be worked out in the blink of an eye in terms of Soul."

"What I mean by this statement is that all karma can generally be worked out by the chela during the second initiation; much during the dream state. There is no need for man to assume that if he has done evil deeds, he will be trapped in these lower planes for ever or even for millions of years."

"This reminds me of the story of Milarepa who, although he practiced black magic and murdered many people, was able to become a great VARDAN Master."

"It was not easy and he had to surrender; but in the end, he became one of the greatest of Masters."

"It has been said that the more checkered and dark the past is for a Soul. The more difficulty and struggle they go through to reach Mastership…the greater a channel they shall be in this world."

"Whether or not this is true, I will say this. Some of the most compassionate VARDAN Masters are those who have suffered the most and had the most difficulty in overcoming obstacles."

"This does not mean our foolishness is a good thing; just that we need not be discouraged as long as we are sincere and willing to make amends and follow the path back home to the source, HURAY, the one true God."

"As said before, ego and vanity are the most difficult of the five passions to overcome. Vanity is the last to go. It overtakes the true self and tries to dominate our lives if we are foolish enough to let it. We can overcome it through its opposite, which is charity and humility to a lesser degree. But the humility I speak of here is not the false humility; that is just another mask of vanity."

"Generally, we can judge our spiritual progress by the fruits of our consciousness. Anyone can speak of humility, charity, chastity, forgiveness and selflessness until the cows come home."

"Talk is cheap. So is action, although less so. What we are alluding to now is consciousness. When a being occupies or is taken over by a particular consciousness, it is as if both heaven and Earth opens up to that consciousness or state of awareness or Beingness; then from that state, all emanates out of the individual. This can be one of the lower states that takes over or one of the higher states. Soul is somewhat like a great mirror."

"Imagine if you will a cave. A dark cavernous cave and the occupants are lighting this cave with small candles that each one carries in their hand."

"This would be the small power of the little self."

"Now imagine that in this cave is a chamber with a hole at the very top, where the sun shines down. And that at high noon, the sun comes streaming down and forms a brilliant beam of light hundreds of thousands, even millions of times brighter, than the candles that they are using to light the cave."

"Now imagine, if you will, that this cave has many other chambers which have no such opening or hole in the ceiling. These chambers are very dark and the people carry these candles so that they can see."

"Now bear with me here my son, for there is a point to this analogy that is of much importance to everyone."

"Imagine that there are mirrors, many mirrors that reflect this light beam from the top of the large chamber where the sun shines down and imagine, that instead of illuminating the cave with the individual candles, each person carries these mirrors and directed the light into the various chambers."

"So that the light did not come from their individual candles, but from the sun itself.

"Now each occupant that carried these mirrors would reflect the light of the sun into various caverns of the cave using this series of mirrors. And how they arranged these mirrors and where they pointed them to illuminate and the size of the beam and whether it was narrow or broad would be entirely up to them."

"This is what Soul faces. IT can use its own illumination and light and sound or it can tap into this endless wellspring of eternal power. The HURAY ITSELF, in the form of the VARDAN Life Stream or Audible Life Stream."

"We each will carry our individual light and sound as the smaller self. This is necessary while in this world. But we have the opportunity to also carry this greater light and sound from the HURAY."

"We need to do both in this world, but we must never put the candle above the sun if we want any hope of being useful to God."

"What we learn is that we are identical in substance to this VARDAN or Life Stream."

"The candle produces light and that light is similar in nature to the light of the sun and yet, the sun is far brighter."

"We may work with the Holy Spirit of God or HURAY and become ITS conscious channels in this world and in all the many levels of heaven and the lower worlds as well."

"We do not have to accept any limitations in our Power, Wisdom, Freedom, nor Love other than our willingness to surrender and in our awareness of that which IS."

"One cannot become God any more than the candle can become the sun."

"But I have said repeatedly, we are not a thing. We are NO Thing. We are pure beingness, pure Soul who has taken on the lower bodies of the etheric, mental, causal, astral and physical in order to work in these coarse vibrations of M.E.S.T. (matter, energy, space, and time.)"

AF: I was suddenly aware that Yaubl Sacabi had something to say and he appeared before us."

YS: "All of this is true, but how does one speak of God or life without speaking a lie? Are not words illusionary being of the Mental Plane and below?"

Rebazar looked at me as if he wanted me to answer Yaubl, but no sooner could I begin to form words, then Yaubl continued.

YS: "It is a rhetorical question" he continued. "But it is the bane of religion. How can God be put inside a box and sold like a box of cracker jacks or cotton candy?"

"Cotton candy is all that man wants really. He wants sugar coated words that make him feel better about his own life and more secure in the afterlife. But as far as security in the afterlife goes, this is ridiculous!

"The only security we may have is if we learn to leave our bodies at will and then we learn to die daily; meaning, we leave our bodies at various times throughout the day and night and visit the various heavenly worlds. Then we experience and overcome so called death! Death is an illusion, but as long as man refuses to leave his body and learn to venture with the aid of the Living VARDAN Master into the higher worlds, man is only fooling himself through religion and the false teachings and dogma of this world."

"Words and more words pile up; emotions and more emotions, feelings of love, community, the things of this world. Thoughts and pretty words and concepts that are neatly packaged in boxes and wrapped in paper with bows tied around them for the eager consumption of the ignorant masses!"

"I say unto you Allen this! Never forget man must awaken to the splendor of the God Worlds of VARDAN. And he must do it in this lifetime and not in the projected future. If he fails in this endeavor, he simply must undergo more incarnations and lower world experiences."

"If man misses the golden opportunity due to distraction from the five passions of the mind, then man must wait; often for centuries or even thousands or hundreds of thousands of years for another opportunity to find the path of Out of Body Tuza Travel."

"It will almost surely be under a different name than VARDANKAR and with a different Master, of course."

"It will most likely have different books or perhaps there will be no books at all on the outer and the Master may operate in secret, due to his particular spiritual mission and the political situation of the times. It is often the case that to practice VARDANKAR publicly was a death sentence, so the VARDAN Masters would have to operate below the radar of society and the church or governmental body preventing free expression."

"The dying daily brings spiritual liberation. What man discovers when he follows the more direct path back to the HURAY is that he existed in these higher worlds all along, but was unaware of this. He learns that he is unfolding spiritually, awakening. He also learns that God and the Margatma or Inner Master have always been with him and are as close as his own heart beat ... in fact closer."

"He was never abandoned by God as it may have appeared from the temporal worlds of illusion or the lower perspective, but has always been loved by the HURAY. Only this love is for his true self Soul. All else has been a creation or dream; or nightmare some might say in jest." (Yaubl smiled softly)

"Man must stop trying to control this world. Cease to be his own worst enemy and start to care about God and about truth."

"Then perhaps he will listen to the Living VARDAN Master of our time and stop playing these senseless games he plays with himself and others. Freedom can never come from the ways of the Kal or negative power; only from the ways of the VARDAN or Spirit."

"The sooner man learns this, the better off he will be spiritually."

"The only thing that VARDAN Masters really ask from man is that he listen to their words and carefully give them weight and evaluate the content of their truth for themselves."

"But man is so engrossed in materiality that he does not even want to listen! He will refuse to listen to the Master, let alone carry out his instructions. So the Master can do little or nothing but must wait until the Soul is more spiritually mature and has learned this particular lesson."

"That the Margatma, the Living VARDAN Master, is the way shower and the sole representative of God in the lower worlds and that he, alone, is the way and means to find the God Head."

"All the other VARDAN Masters must bow before him, not because he is superior in any way, but because he has the Rod of VARDAN Power and as such, this forms a conduit of light and sound or a grounding point, where Souls can step into his field or aura or sphere of influence and be carried on it, a bit like the transporter beams in the TV show Star Trek."

"The second the Master gives up this rod of power, he is then simply a member of the order of the Bourchakoun."

"It is not him in the personality that is great. It is the primal VARDAN using him as ITS vehicle to bring Souls back home."

"Man does not seem to understand this and begins either rejecting the Margatma, the Living VARDAN Master or trying to worship him as a personality figure or some sort of deity."

"Although he tries to discourage this, it is found that some of his more immature chelas will not understand this spiritual nature and try and put him as Jesus, on a pedestal above his fellow man."

"In the flesh, he is ordinary. It is only spiritually that he possesses this rod of power and it is the rod of power that brings Souls home, through the direction of the Soul who is given the possession of it."

"It is much like what Rebazar described with the cave and mirrors. The mirrors reflecting the rays of the sun into the dark cave."

"Without this Rod of power, the Soul whose job it was to bring Souls back to the God worlds would fail in his mission, because he would not possess the necessary Power, Wisdom, Freedom and Love. It is only through this Rod of Power that Souls can be brought forth and overcome their own downward pull from countless past lives."

"I don't know how to make this any more clear."

17

KATA DAKI TALKS ABOUT LOVE

I have had many wondrous encounters with the great VARDAN Master Kata Daki. She has come to me many times when I was in distress. Although this book is titled Dialogues with the Masters, there was one time I would like to share with you to illustrate a point and give more background. It was a past life I had hundreds of years ago. I lived in the beautiful countryside of Greece on my own plot of land with my then wife and three lovely young children. My wife and I were relatively young and our children, two lovely girls I seem to recall 4 and 6 and our boy who was 8, made a splendid family. Or at least so I thought.

We were farmers and the soil on the lush land was dark black in color. There where trees and grass everywhere and our garden yielded lots of vegetables which we ate and sold a few in the market for money of which we needed very little being almost self-sufficient.

I loved my family and I loved my little cottage and garden. I loved everything about them. I realize now that each person has a unique way that they accept God's love into their lives. This unique way or ways allows them to accept a certain degree of love and charity from the VARDAN or spirit and from God.

For me, I would partake of God's love and blessings through my family, home, the garden and mother nature.

My wife and I had an argument when we had first acquired the land.

I agreed that I would build us a small house. I would do almost all the work myself with some help from her. I decided quickly that I would build our home out of wood. There were many trees on our property as well as in the nearby forest and I thought a nice wood house would be perfect for our needs. My wife, on the other hand, had a different idea. She wanted me to build our home out of stone.

I did not like this idea at all! First of all, I imagined having to carry almost countless stones long distances or pay money we did not have, to have others do this for me. Secondly, I did not know as much about stone work as working with wood so it would be harder in every way for me to do this. I scoffed at her idea, saying that she would be happy with a nice wood house and to trust me. To be honest, it just seemed like too much trouble and I was lazy and did not see the need, although later I would understand why she wanted the house out of stone and not wood.

We argued about it and she really seemed to want it out of stone…but I would not budge. Since I was going to do most of the work and was the man in the house, I would decide and her arguments were not strong enough to motivate me to change my mind. I did not understand, until much later why she seemed so fervent on having a stone house and I don't think she consciously knew either. But she had a feeling, but could not articulate it in a logical argument that would convince me otherwise.

It was not until years later that I would discover why.

Every few weeks to a month or two, I would go out into the markets to acquire things that we needed but could not easily get in the country. These were short trips. I would be gone perhaps three or four days. I had been doing this for years and it was nothing out of the ordinary.

I left for such a trip and the trip went fine. I acquired some rope, fabric and other items and even had some gold and silver coins from trading some of our things at market.

However when I arrived back home, what I saw was for me unimaginable.

Having derived all my love in life from my family and home, what I saw was that my house had burned down to the ground and worst of all I found the charred bodies of my wife and children lying in the burnt rubble.

I was speechless and went into shock. I thought I had lost everything worth living for.

I stayed there for two long days not sure if my eyes deceived me, but studying the grossly burnt bodies I knew they once were my family.

Finally after two or three days, I completely and utterly gave up on life. I did not kill myself but I no longer wanted to remain on Earth.

All the love I had from God and the VARDAN, it seemed, had come in the form of my family, home and garden. Now that it was all gone, I felt I had nothing to live for.

Being so depressed, I ate very little food…and what little I did eat was poor. I simply did not care about life. All appeared lost. I truly thought that God had forsaken me and life was no longer worth living.

My life became one of deep sadness. I built a small shack to keep the rain off of me and keep me warm. It was nailed together and small. I simply did not care anymore. I did not take care of myself. I saw no reason.

Others in my village, although few in number, tried to console me but it was of no use. I felt as if I had totally died and that all of God's love had been cut or severed from my life and I had no love to live upon. Life seemed pointless.

It was during this time that Kata Daki, who is an ancient VARDAN Master, appeared to me on the inner in order to try and console me.

What I did not understand was that the VARDAN or Holy Spirit was trying to give me a higher form of love than my family and country home.

The light and sound was flowing in gentle waves beckoning me to accept it and let go of my attachment to my dead family and previous life.

But I was so attached to them that I would not let go. I was so attached to that particular form of love, the embodiment of love in the form of my previous life before the fire, that I could or would not let go of that form of love. I would not accept any other form than the one I had previously enjoyed and accepted.

I was more attached to form and did not recognize that God's love, in the form of the Audible Life Stream or VARDAN, was beckoning me to accept an even greater love than what I had previously experienced.

Kata Daki tried to comfort me on the inner. She appeared to

me and gave me great compassion. She has honey blond hair and wore a maroon robe. She appeared in her early 30s although she is very ancient. She still appears the same as she did back then, although this was hundreds of years earlier. She often appears to those, who are undergoing severe hardship, to comfort them and give them solace and compassion.

I was such a person, for I had blamed myself for the death of my family. This was part of the problem. The enormous guilt that I felt, along with the deep sadness.

Had I built the house out of stone, like my wife begged me to do, I imagine none of this would have happened.

I did not know how the fire started, only that my family was dead and now God had abandoned me, and life without their love and the love I felt from being in my previous existence had sustained me and made me feel this love in powerful waves of contentment, peace and serenity.

Now it was all gone and in its place was hardship, sadness, guilt and a meaningless life of remorse.

Yes, I was feeling very sorry for myself indeed. I was very attached to the pain and guilt and deep longing and sadness I was experiencing.

Kata Daki tried. I was seeing a wonderful blue light: that of the Margatma or blue light of VARDAN. This is the light that illuminates the path back to God.

I was hearing the inner sound current beckoning me to surrender and move into higher states of awareness where I could have experienced a far greater love then before.

But I could only see my own selfish pain and was trapped by

my own inability to see past the pain and attachment to my guilt and family.

I had become so attached to the love of God being expressed in this particular way, in the form of my wife, young children, nature and farm house; that anything else was unthinkable.

I would not listen to Kata Daki. I was too attached and depressed and guilty, that I failed to pass the test of wanting truth and God above the things of this world.

I ended up dying an early death from self neglect. I lived for perhaps another 12 long years and died young and depressed. Some would say I died from a broken heart. But it was also that I did not take care of myself properly, did not keep warm enough in the winter; did not feed myself good enough food, nor did I find much joy in the remainder of my life.

I had missed the opportunity from Kata Daki and from the HURAY Itself and the VARDAN, ITS voice, to accept ITS love and find comfort in the VARDAN.

Because of my failure to do this, I would need to learn the lesson that one cannot pick and choose the way God's love and the spirit or VARDAN gives one ITS blessings.

Life is always hard for those who pick and choose. We must surrender and then the VARDAN and Master will give us all that we need in the form that is best for the good of the whole.

If we cling to our forms and old understandings; we become like I was back in old time Greece: attached, disillusioned and unhappy.

We cannot afford to stand in the way of our own spiritual

progress by trying to control the God Power or VARDAN. We must surrender to IT and let go of our own human little self and our petty concerns long enough, to leave our physical bodies and venture into the worlds above matter, energy, time and space.

Kata Daki began to speak. Her presence was light and filled with a great love and compassion which I was very aware came from the HURAY Worlds and the great Ocean of Love and Mercy.

KD: "It is good you have told that story. It was a long time ago and you have learned much since then about letting go of all forms that do not support your spiritual mission and the good of the whole."

"What is love? That is the question."

"Who can define love in words, but we must try so I will begin this discourse with this to say."

"Love is demonstrated in our outflow of consciousness."

"There are essentially two parts to love, actually three, but most only know of two."

"They are:
1. Inflow.
2. Outflow
3. That part of love that cannot be expressed nor spoken of in any way. The inner side of love, much like the inner side of Soul or the inner side of the HURAY. Also called the Dhunatmik. Although some call it Nirguna which is a more accurate description of the Inner side of the HURAY!"

Note: The Voice of the HURAY contains two parts, the

168

Varnatmik and the Dhunatmik. The Varnatmik is that part of the Audible life Stream that can be spoken of and has many attributes, including Love, Wisdom, Power and Freedom. The Dhunatmik is the inner side of the VARDAN that nothing can be said about.

K.D. "Often, man must learn to give before he can receive. He must become, as Paulji and other VARDAN Masters have said before him, a magnet of love. He must emanate this love outward and then it begins to return unto him. He cannot emanate this love with the idea that he will use it for selfish purposes ... then it becomes selfish love which is a form of human love or love of the little self or Kal."

"No, he must give without thinking of reward. Love simply for the sake of love. Of course, I am speaking here of divine love and not human love. Divine love could be expressed as good will toward all and in divine love, there is hope for man. It is not only unselfish love but unconditional love and being unconditional, he does not ask for anything in return but simply loves as the sun shines down upon the Earth without asking for anything in return."

"When we practice this divine love or good will towards all beings and life in all worlds, including the physical world, we begin to find immortality. But we must be careful that we focus on loving God or the HURAY, the Living VARDAN Master and the VARDAN of ITSELF. If we love the things of this world or direct our love in an attached way or try and serve individuals by attempting to serve our fellow man, we shall fail in our duties to God."

"We must become conscious channels or vehicles for HURAY'S love and divine blessings. We do this partly through declaring ourselves a channel for the HURAY, Margatma and VARDAN."

"We must do this with total sincerity."

"It is said that those who chase God find God flees from them!"

"Why is this? Because God is already in our presence we need only become aware of IT. Soul exists simultaneously in all worlds, including the Anami Lok and even the secret dwelling place of the HURAY, the Ocean of Love and Mercy or 12th plane, two planes above the Anami Lok."

"We can become aware, but it is generally a process of initiation and doing our spiritual exercises on a daily basis, that brings us to truth."

"The inflow is another matter since it is that wave that emanates and sustains all life, all beings and all worlds upon worlds."

"But it is the following of the returning wave that reflects back to God that brings us truth."

"We cannot find truth in the sustaining wave that issues down into these lower worlds, but must ride the returning wave."

"As you and the other Masters have stated Allen, the VARDAN or Audible Life Stream flows downward and sustains all the many universes of God, from the highest to the lowest. Each time it lowers in vibratory rate, a new lord or ruler is lay manifest, who then acts as a transformer or channel to sustain all below ITS world."

"But none of these rulers are God; only lords or rulers."

"Once Soul reaches the first of the lower worlds, the current splits into positive and negative. Fractures like a prism or rainbow into many different sub currents or forces. This is why there is so much confusion. The Souls living in these lower worlds must take on various lower bodies, including a mind, emotions and of course a physical body."

"When the wave of VARDAN travels downward it sustains, but finally the wave reaches the very bottom and begins to travel upward in an ascending wave."

"This is the wave, as I have said, that Soul must grab onto in order to reach perfection or Self and God Realization."

"When we die daily, we are uplifted into these high, high worlds through the love and blessings of the Living VARDAN Master and through the HURAY ITSELF."

"Since you are the Master as of this moment, you may be wondering why you feel so imperfect."

"This is good for you must remain humble; it is only your inner self that is perfect, never the little self our outer ego self."

"When one participates in this love, this wave that ascends upward; they become a light unto the world."

"The VARDAN Masters are all lights onto this world, for they bring man to this ascending wave and this is the highest form of love there is!!!"

"Do you understand now? Man is so busy trying to define and qualify and quantify and codify love, that he misses love entirely. This is sort of what you did in Greece after that tragic fire."

"The whole thing was arranged by God or the spirit or VARDAN.

"Your family agreed that they would leave this world early so that you would have the opportunity to choose and learn the difference between form and pure love."

"Love has many faces and those who pick and choose what form they will take and what form they will reject are not wise individuals and will, in effect, eventually cut themselves off to a degree from love."

"We cannot, for example, decide we will only give love to people who are good looking or people between certain ages or from certain ethnic backgrounds, without undergoing hardships at some point in time."

"We may see love in the form of the inner light or hear love as the inner sound. These are from the Holy Spirit or VARDAN and give us the opportunity to follow this love and follow the Master."

"But most reject this sort of love, because it lacks in the flashiness of the lower worlds."

"The humble light and sound of HURAY may not appear blinding nor the sound as enchanting as one would imagine."

"Sometimes it comes as the still whisper in the night. When we least expect it. When we least expect love."

"It comes in a form most do not recognize, for it is stepped down in vibration to that level we can understand and handle it at."

"If the light and sound were to come full force, it would only delay our journey back to God. It would be far too much. Like having the entire ocean dumped into a swimming pool would wipe out an entire surrounding state and do no one any good."

"Therefore, we must go in gradual increments and establish ourselves in those states of consciousness we are ready to expand into. This is part of the purpose of the VARDAN Golden Wisdom Temples where, on each plane, a Master is in charge of that temple and the souls there study the Shariyat-Ki-HURAY."

"Love, my friend, is a deep and some say mysterious topic, but it is only mysterious to those who cannot leave their bodies and travel into the higher worlds. In the higher worlds above the mental and etheric planes beyond time, space and mind, there are no questions; only understanding in the form of direct perception: Seeing, Knowing and Being."

"This is the whole point of the VARDANKAR teachings and why so few will ever understand them."

"It requires a letting go of all that we think we know, so that truth and divine love may enter our hearts and minds.

"Eventually, we discover that we are truth. The living, breathing truth and that all love, wisdom, power and freedom belongs to Soul, our true self, and the only difference between Souls is in the degree of realization and expansion of consciousness that they possess.

"Then we cease to compare ourselves with others and know that we are a law unto ourselves."

"Thus we follow the great law known as the law of love. We find in the end that we are the VARDAN of ITSELF and that the VARDAN is LOVE, therefore we are LOVE."

"Of course, we are far more than just LOVE but in the end this LOVE or more accurately DIVINE LOVE, grabs a hold of us since it is that part of us that is eternal and we ride this wave back home to God."

"That is all for today."

"Know that I love you."

18

YAUBL SACABI ON TRUTH

YS: "Man needs to stop thinking, stop reading, stop feeling and start being. The sooner he does this the better. He does this through surrender and the letting go of his opinions and dogma and the realization that he is not a thing but a Great Soul who is, in a sense, one with the VARDAN and Master.

"Then he practices the spiritual exercises of VARDANKAR according to the Master's inner and outer instructions and finds great success in leaving the body and dwelling in those worlds beyond time and space."

"VARDANKAR is not taught; it is caught."

"Do not try and think your way into heaven; you will only fail in this."

"Instead, stop trying to do anything! Don't is eternal to Being."

"BEING is in the moment. It is in the here and now. Doing projects into the future or past and is mechanical. BEING is in the ISNESS of God. Doing is in the realm of mind, feeling and physical action."

"This does not mean we do not study, read and contemplate the VARDAN works. It does not mean we become passive in nature. It means we do without doing; think without thinking."

"We become detached and recognize that we carry around these Kal bodies in order to interact with this world and the various lower worlds, but we are not these lower bodies therefore we remain detached to them. If they act up on us, we need not identify with them. We become almost like the man with a remote control airplane, who flies it with a sense of watching and detachment. He recognizes that the airplane, while an extension of himself, is not himself, only a remote control flying device."

"When we become detached, we can begin to take responsibility for our own state of consciousness and work for the universal cause."

"At first, this will be helping the Master with his spiritual mission. Eventually, we will reach our own states of God Realization and VARDAN Mastership. We will still help the Living VARDAN Master, but now we find we have more freedom because we are more responsible, aware and conscious. When a being is conscious, they are alive and less mechanical in nature. They reach total awareness and enter the pure states of Seeing, Knowing and Being and know all things through direct perception. This does not mean we should become vain and egotistical."

"I am speaking here of Soul, not the lower bodies. In the lower bodies, we are imperfect and subject to mistakes and accidents."

"We are in the worlds of the Kal."

"So, truth is a matter of ceasing to become absorbed in one's attention on the things of the Kal or negative; and placing it upon the Master, VARDAN and HURAY."

"Truth is a matter of consciousness, of course and also attention and to a lesser degree, imagination."

"Soul sees through imagination in the lower worlds."

"In the higher worlds, Soul has direct perception and requires no mind whatsoever."

"In the lower worlds, we must work with imagination, emotion; but most of all attention which is a form of imagination and thought."

"Those who control their attention are generally powerful individuals, but those who not only control their attention but choose to place it upon the VARDAN, Inner Master and HURAY are indeed wise and will, in time, become a VARDAN Master themselves."

"Attention is like a mighty spotlight or searchlight that illuminates. It is also capable of listening and focusing upon the Sound Current or Audible Life Stream."

"Through attention, one may become aware of the presence of the Inner Master and carry on conversations with him or any of the other VARDAN Masters such as Rebazar Tarzs, myself, Fubbi Quantz and so forth."

"Truth, while it cannot be defined nor really spoken about except in a rather vague way, must give way to the experience of truth. And this experience often comes through the use of imagination, attention and focus. When we have laser like focus, we begin to gain control over our own states of consciousness. We must learn and develop clever ways of leaving our bodies and venturing into the other worlds and meeting with the VARDAN Masters on the Inner planes and Golden Wisdom Temples."

"Until we learn to do this, we are not progressing very fast on the path. But it can be learned if we stop becoming our own worst enemy and failing to have faith and clinging to our own ideas and opinions about truth, even when they have failed us time and time again..."

"Man must be humble and surrender to the VARDAN and to his True Self, his eternal God self. First and foremost, he must learn to surrender to the Inner Master and the other VARDAN Masters with total humility."

"He must give up his struggles and problems to the Master." "THIS MUST BE DONE if he is to make any real progress on the path. If he resists, things will only get delayed."

"It is the turning over of the inner tensions and problems to the Master that frees one to use his Tuza energy to break free of this world. Until then, man is in a constant struggle for survival and for the things of this world. He is at war with himself, at war with everything and everyone."

"He does not know where to turn. He turns left and there is trouble, right and also. Only when he walks the middle path of VARDANKAR and turns over his inner life to the VARDAN and Master, does he see true progress ... until then, nothing much will become of him."

"All the riches and fame of the world will do man no good if he cannot find God. All the praise, health, human love, honors and friendships mean nothing if he has lost himself in order to find the things of this world."

"What does it profit a man to gain the entire world if he loses his Soul?"

"What difference does it mean for a man to be King for 40 or 80 years if, at the end of it, he translates and must come back into these lower worlds again and again, with nothing much to show for his troubles?"

"Most men will argue that they can make the world a better place. They can serve their fellow man. Help him eat food, give him comfort and love. This may be true. A man may provide food for his entire community. He may give out deeds of charity and honor. He may become a great teacher of material and emotional education and teach his fellow man about the lower worlds from his meager understanding, in order to improve the conditions under which they live. But this is only temporary."

"He is not feeding them the spiritual light and sound, the VARDAN. He is not giving them the true Wisdom of the God worlds. He is only teaching them certain principles that can be gleaned from the lower wisdom, of the lower worlds of time and space."

"When it is all over, he will find he did not make a real difference in their lives. That they and he will have to incarnate at some point and start again. Always, the real test is: does one want God or does one want the things of this world?"

"If one claims they desire God but, in reality, they only desire physical, emotional and mental comforts and materiality, then none who is of the higher states of consciousness will believe them. They will know he is not a true spiritual seeker but a part of the ignorant masses, who do not seek truth but only the things of this world. They seek women, wine, happiness and contentment. They seek good health and abundance of a material and emotional nature. They seek a lesser God. One who will grant them wishes much like a mighty genie, as in Aladdin's lamp, who will grant them countless wishes simply by them asking."

"This is the worst sort of materialism there is, for it is disguised as spirituality!"

"One may pretend they are spiritual, but how can one truly be spiritual if they shun God? How can one claim to want to know truth and yet be fearful of leaving their physical body and seeking truth?"

"Can one find it in books? In lectures? In the things of this world? Does truth exist in the embrace of a woman's love? Or in the face of a child? Or in the glitter of gold and precious jewels?"

"Yes and no, I say unto you. There is nothing wrong with human love nor material wealth other than the fact that it shall not, nor never will replace the seeking of God! And contrary to what most claim, God cannot be brought into the material world for God does not dwell here. Yes, there is the VARDAN that is stepped down in order to sustain these lower worlds but one cannot find God in this world of materialism; but must learn to leave the physical body and venture out into the far country."

"Seek first the kingdom of God and all will be given unto thee! These are words of wisdom, for all who are true to God know this."

"But again, we are not speaking of the God of materiality, the Kal Niranjan or the Brahm, who often appears to man as a mighty being with a shining white rob and beard. Others may see him as a white light and his face is said to be so beautiful that once one sees him they cannot look away. They are struck with such awe that they are often left speechless and totally convinced that he is God and they have finally found truth! They desire to dwell in his world for all of eternity and are usually convinced that this is the goal of life."

"What they fail to understand is that this is just the Brahm. He is only a ruler of the lower worlds, mainly the causal and mental planes. In a sense, he is the universal mind power and as such, he is the father and mother of all minds."

"He, of course, possesses great powers for he sustains all the worlds below him. He creates or manifests. Actually, manifestation is all that he can do for creation is finished in the lower worlds of time and space, but anyway, he manifests and from out of him many things come. The powers that pour forth from the higher worlds have been split up into positive, negative and neutral forces, when they enter the lower worlds of opposites and M.E.S.T.!"

"It is much like a prism or rainbow that splits the light of the sun into almost countless colors or shades of violet, blue, yellow, red, orange, green and so forth."

"Likewise, there are many forces or sub-currents necessary in order to manifest matter, energy, space and time; in order to make up the molecules and atoms that exist in this world; the life functions of the various lower bodies; the powers split up and split up again, until we find they settle in the human body which is little more than a machine."

"Even the mind is, in actuality, just a highly complex machine.

"It is only the VARDAN or spirit that animates all of life and makes it real. All but the HURAY is an illusion.

"So, perhaps, you see the folly of worshiping a ruler and mistaking him for the HURAY or one true God?

"Most men do not understand what I speak of here. So listen closely. Soul does not work in the field of time and space. Soul is not limited in any way. Soul knows through direct perception: Seeing, Knowing and Being.

"Soul is that mighty drop from the Ocean of Love and Mercy that has no bounds other than its own awareness."

"Soul does not contain any negativity; only the pure positive God Force from the HURAY. Soul is identical in substance to the VARDAN that pure positive Sound Current, the Audible Life Stream. It contains all Love, Wisdom, Power and Freedom and beyond!

"And yet, you ask how can man become so negative?

"It is the lower bodies that Soul takes on in order to experience these lower worlds for Soul's education!"

"It is said in the Shariyat-Ki-HURAY, the holy book of VARDANKAR, that when Souls existed in the high worlds of God, they were unconscious. They played and frolicked but did not give to one another. They were not spiritually mature nor growing in conscious awareness."

"The HURAY, in its humble abode, saw this and using the great sound and light issued a command and suddenly a series of worlds began to be created as the VARDAN or light and sound issued out like a mighty radio wave moving outward."

"As this beacon descended in vibratory rate, another manifestation of the HURAY was created at correspondingly lower and lower vibrations. These manifestations were, in fact, mighty rulers who channeled the power to all below them!"

"This continued until world upon world had been created, but then it could go no lower."

"So, by the command of the mighty HURAY, the great Sat Nam, the lord of the Atma Lok or Soul plane, also known as the 5th plane split the pure positive force into two streams. And thus, the first of the true lower worlds were created."

"This event cascaded down as each succeeding ruler created a plane below him until, we find, we are at the bottom of the heap so to speak in this physical world which, quite frankly, is the ash can of the universe known as Earth or the Earth world."

"The Souls who were unconscious were then cast out of their true home, the Ocean of Love and Mercy and found themselves taking on the various lower bodies. The etheric or subconscious body, the mental or mind body, the causal or memory body, the astral or emotional body and, of course, the physical body."

"Soul was now forced to receive an education so that one day it would return to the great HURAY but, this time, with the proper education and experiences, so that it would take its place as a conscious co-worker throughout Eternity."

"This has been and always will be the divine plan and no one can stop it. We may try and delay the returning of ourselves to the HURAY, but we cannot stop it any more than we can stop the Earth's sun from finally burning out and causing the death of this planet."

"The truth is that God does not really care when man

returns back to IT: only that Soul returns. The HURAY does not care if it takes 1 second or 1 billion years for a Soul to return. The HURAY exists in eternity and, as such, there is no time nor space. Nor does the HURAY care about lower embodiments; it only cares about Soul who is eternal, unchanging, indestructible, and cannot be burned, broken, pierced nor harmed in any way shape or form."

"It is only the lower bodies of man, such as the astral and physical bodies, that can be damaged.

"So man has a choice."

Yaubl began to pace up and down which was unusual for him.

Y. S. "Now I want to point something out here that is important."

"I had said that the HURAY does not care how long it takes Soul to return to it. But this is one of the great paradoxes of the world. All exists within the confines of eternity and, of course, eternity contains NO confines of any sort!"

Yaubl laughed, as if telling a joke and I smiled.

Y. S. "Anyway, moving along, since man exists in the here and now, the HURAY had a problem ... if you could call it that. Of course, the HURAY does not have problems but I don't know what else to call it other than a problem."

"You see, while IT did not care ... it did want Soul to return. And since Soul exists beyond time and space the HURAY provided a way shower so that those Souls, who were ready, did not have to suffer needlessly on the 'wheel of 84.'"

"I know this is complicated but it is really quite simple ... see the mind works as a computer. Things are either true or false. But the spiritual path does not work this way at all. It works with conscious awareness, the conscious awareness of each Soul and various states of consciousness. So we have the macrocosm and the microcosm."

"The microcosm is man's own world and state of consciousness. The macrocosm is the universal spirit of VARDAN which contains the whole which one can place no limitations upon therefore it is always in expansion."

"Our microcosm is also in expansion as well. The two are on parallel fields, the microcosm and the macrocosm."

So perhaps you see that the higher one goes spiritually, the less difference there is between the microcosm and the macrocosm?"

AF: "I have to say this is a bit confusing to me."

YS: "Of course. Do you have any questions?"

AF: "How does one apply this?"

YS: "Hum ... this is a good question. I do not know."

AF: "Master, I am confused."

YS: "Yes."

There was a long pause as I wondered what the point of all this really was.

Y.S. "Okay. So maybe you can see it now? That the reconciliation of the microcosm with the macrocosm is one of man's greatest challenges! Man believes falsely that he is in a sort of war or conflict between the universal all and himself!"

"He thinks in a strange sense that he is in conflict with God!"

"How strange this is!"

"But this is all a product of the universal mind power at its highest level of differentiation. You see this conflict is of the mind."

"The mind must divide things into the field of opposites, good and evil, mountains and valleys, positive and negative, love and hate, inside and outside, them and me. So on and so forth!"

"The mind is, as I said, like a very complicated computer or machine with many moving parts that are actually powered by the VARDAN as electricity powers a motor."

"The mind gives the illusion of separation or identification."

"Now it is true that Soul always retains its individuality, so what I am not saying is we will get absorbed into some cosmic ocean and lose our individuality!"

"I am not saying that at all mind you, simply this: that the mind cannot understand this apparent conflict. It needs to be black and white in order for the mind to process. The mind needs to try and separate things into the field of opposites."

"Soul, on the other hand, does not exist in this field of opposites. It is independent of them. Has nothing to do with them."

"This is one reason why man needs his lower bodies to operate in the lower worlds. Are you beginning to understand yet?"

AF: "I think so."

YS: "Good."

AF: "Why can't we simply experience the Beingness, Knowingness and Seeingness of the higher worlds and the direct perception from Soul? What is the benefit of understanding the inner workings of the Mind?"

YS: "This question is kind of obvious but I will try and answer you anyway. In order to live in this world and be of use here in these lower worlds, Soul must take control or, more accurately, custody of the mind and other lower bodies. Until this is done, we run the danger of having these lower bodies out-create us!"

"I wish to continue with this important discourse. Now discipline or lack of discipline often comes from the lack of understanding this simple concept of opposites of the microcosm and the macrocosm and the division between mind and Soul."

"There is a sort of war going on inside most men. It is a war for the self, the true self. Will the mind and lower bodies win or Soul? Mostly, the lower bodies temporarily win. This has always been the case since the beginning of time long before recorded history."

"This is because the lower bodies exist in the lower worlds and are, at times, overwhelmingly real, while Soul and the VARDAN are more subtle.

"This subtlety does not mean the VARDAN is not powerful; simply that the vibratory rate of divine spirit is much higher than the vibratory rate of the lower bodies therefore the lower bodies are more dense."

"I guess a crude analogy is the difference between hitting air and hitting water."

"If one flies into air at 80 miles per hour, they will feel the air moving against their body strongly."

"If one were to fly into water at 80 miles per hour, it would kill them because the water is much denser then air."

"If the air were moving at only ½ mile per hour, they might barely feel it at all. Water moving ½ mile per hour, on the other hand, would be quite noticeable when compared to the air."

"Man does not seem to be able to stop thinking and this is fine. What we do is not stop thinking. No this is wrong. We may allow the mind to think all it wants. The mind is a necessary tool while in the lower worlds. What we do is simply control our attention. We allow the mind to carry on with some discipline, but we place our attention upon the Inner Master and the Audible Life Stream or VARDAN light and sound."

"This is what we must do. Any other method will simply not work."

"Let the mind chatter. We may let it go on if we choose to and not worry so much about it. It is of little concern to us for it's like a small child playing in the garden. It digs up things and throws them around but we need not worry too much about it."

"When it becomes unruly, we may have to discipline it but, for the most part, we simply learn detachment."

"The mind flows in grooves like a record player follows the grooves cut out in the vinyl. If anyone remembers the old vinyl records any more, they had grooves cut into them with a tiny diamond. I believe it was a diamond. When the needle was put onto the groove, it had no choice but to follow that groove and play whatever was impressed into that groove by the needle that was used to record the sound."

"So the mind is little more than a machine and, as such, we simply make contact with the VARDAN and the VARDAN will help us deal with the mind if we will simply place our attention upon the VARDAN and Inner Master, or one of the true Spiritual Travelers."

"Then we find we begin to unlock this whole mystery about opposites and the microcosm and the macrocosm, and this war between the little self and the greater self soon begins to wind down, as we give it less attention and give more to the Master."

"This is the way it should be. The placing of one's imagination and attention upon what we want rather than on what we do not want!"

"Simple isn't it? Or do you find it complicated?"

A.F. "No it is simple Master, but it seems harder to put into practice then to speak of it?"

Y. S. "Yes, perhaps. If you believe it's hard, then it shall be hard for you. If you believe it is easy, then the obstacles become no big deal; only part of the process culminating in your eventual victory!!!"

"One man curses his mistakes and curses his failures."

"Another man blesses his mistakes and blesses his failures."

"Why? Because the first man is looking at them as curses and failures. The second man does not view them so much as mistakes but as learning experiences."
"The second man secretly harbors in his very heart and Beingness, the knowledge that he will find truth."

"The first man harbors resentment, feelings of inadequacy, disillusionment and the feeling that no matter what he does, he will fail at it."

"What is the difference between these two?

"The first man is still not ready for God while the second is."

"That is all. Not that one is better than the other; simply that one man is afraid of his own divinity and the other embraces it."

"I say this to you and everyone reading."

"You are your own worst enemy and your own best friend. You are a two-edged sword. One will strike the chains that bind you and cut them in half like twigs. The other side of this sword will cut your hand off in a single blow."

"You must temper your imaginative facility until it is sharper then the finest samurai sword ... then still sharper."

"You must develop an iron will to find truth and God, no matter the cost."

"You must develop sincerity and fear nothing and let nothing stand between you and truth."

"You must become selfless and humble before the Master and before God ITSELF. Then and only then will you understand what I have said today."

And with that, the great Yaubl Sacabi disappeared.

19

HOW THE IMAGINATION OF MAN HELPS SHAPE HIS REALITY: PART ONE

I had been feeling rather lost with my life. The conditions of my life were such that there were times when I wondered how long I would continue to live in this world. It was a time of great hardship and I often wondered whether I would ever get VARDANKAR out to this dark dreary world. It seemed many times I might lose my physical body and would run out of time in this world. This seemed to be the nature of life on Earth and the other planets of the physical world. Souls need bodies as vehicles of expression because Soul of ITSELF, like God in a sense, has far too high a vibration to interact with the lower worlds, without the various bodies such as the astral, causal and physical.

It was in this state of mind that I once again had the pleasure of meeting with Rebezar Tarzs, who's wisdom and brilliance are an inspiration to all Souls desiring truth and a way home to the source of all and home of Soul, the Anami Lok and beyond into the true Ocean of Love and Mercy; where IT the HURAY of ITSELF exists and Soul may not only find its father and true home, but find its spiritual mission and become a conscious co-worker throughout eternity.

RT: "I wish now to speak on imagination, if this is OK?"

AF: "Yes, of course."

RT: "The title of this discourse is How Imagination Helps Shape Man's Reality. It is a good one so listen up."

"I cannot tell you how many chelas get lost in this world of time and space because they allow their minds and emotions or that part of man known loosely as the astral body, to out-create him through his vivid imagination!"

"What man imagines is real becomes real! This is one of the hidden laws of the universe. The metaphysicians have been preaching this for centuries, no thousands upon thousands of years. Dare they stop, they would have nothing else to talk about!"

"But we must go further than this. This is just a base understanding. In order to be useful, we must become masters of imagination and actually transcend imagination into that which we call Tuza or Soul Travel!"

"Enter VARDANKAR, the Ancient Science of Tuza Travel!"

"It is here we begin to see just how Soul creates its own realities and they exist layer upon layer, like rings inside of a great tree of life."

"There is almost no end to these layers of reality but they are, for the most part, of a false nature and yield not truth but illusion and disillusion."

"See, when man bases his reality upon time and space, matter and energy and prays to his space God for his salvation, he is really missing the boat spiritually. He is lost without the God-man or Spiritual Traveler in his life ... but most men are fools and do not know this, or refuse to recognize this due to their insincerity and ignorance of truth and God's ways."

"These varied layers of false realities are made up of many things too numerous to completely cover here."

"I have spoken of how the spiritual current of the VARDAN splits into positive, negative and neutral, forming the worlds of duality."

"This is important information that most do not understand but think they do. At the point of splitting, we begin to get many varied streams of conscious awareness and power."

"The energy splits again and again forming seemingly countless currents and sub-currents until it becomes almost unbearably confusing for the mind of man to comprehend."

"For example, the various energy streams that are responsible in forming life on Earth and maintaining it are almost beyond belief. There are nature spirits and other lower beings, whose job it is to maintain the processes of the lower worlds regarding the life and death of plants and animals at the cellular, as well as systematic level."

"This is true of all of man's bodies. When the Mountain of Light on the Astral Plane pours out its great current of light and sound upon the Astral and Physical planes of existence, all shake and tremble except the spiritual travelers and those Souls who know this is not the beginning of creation, but only the Astral World."

"These fractured currents have almost countless colors and sounds."

"The mind itself has a complexity as it filters through these currents that sustain various processes, including but not limited to, the processes of reincarnation and to a lesser extent karma!"

"How could this be? Does not man believe that God ITSELF is involved in all of this? That it is a personal thing?"

"Well my son, it is and it is not as they say. It really has more to do with imagination."

"Soul in the lower worlds is a bit like a painter with countless colors and brushes at his disposal upon which to choose his form of expressions."

"Man must choose what energies he wishes to channel or if he desires to free himself of all of this impurity and be a conscious channel for only the highest God has to offer."

"We can either become a minor messenger of the energies and forces of the Kal and Brahm or we can become a great channel for the VARDAN and Master."

"We can get caught in the sub-planes of the Astral, Causal or Mental regions of the lower worlds or follow the great Spiritual Travelers of VARDANKAR and bring ourselves in consciousness into the light and sound of God."

"Are we sincere in finding God or are we insincere and only desire to partake, using our imaginations, of the lower forces of nature and the universal mind power?"

"I say images along with these fractured streams of consciousness make up all life for the fool who refuses truth."

"For those who embrace truth and the true spiritual travelers, life is made out of divine consciousness and the VARDAN or light and sound, the Audible Life Stream, the source of all, the God power emanating out of the true

HURAY dwelling in the Ocean of Love and Mercy."

"This is the pure positive sound current and contains all things. It is the source from which all Souls came from and all Souls will return in time and beyond time, to their true home there."

"But in the meantime, Souls may play in these lower worlds with the dual forces of the lower realities, such as love and hate, mountains and valleys, good and evil and time and space."

"The wise Soul recognizes two things."

1. That IT is not its picture files or engrams from the countless past lives it has experienced in the lower worlds.

2. That the almost countless sub-currents coming from the Kal Power are not truth but only a reflection of a reflection of a reflection of truth and that truth can only be known through leaving one's body and boldly venturing into the higher worlds beyond matter, energy, space and time.

"I say this unto you all. Man is fractured. He is a fractured creature who is mechanical in nature. But man has a Soul and this is his true self. His Soul is indestructible and does not really need the lower self, except to gain experience in these lower worlds."

"But the little self or mechanical self of man needs Soul, because Soul is the only part of it that is real and Soul animates all of man's lower bodies."

"So, of course, we are Soul. That is our true God self, our only self. But this false self or ego self gets in the way and causes trouble for us through the undisciplined mind."

"The five passions rule over those with an undisciplined mind and this must end if man is to find truth in its entirety, if such a thing were even possible!"

"Man gets in his own way. He is his own worst enemy. He clings to his own meager understandings and will generally not listen to the words of the Margatma, the Living VARDAN Master of his time. If he did listen, he would have a chance at making the journey back to God, but he fails in this because of his attachment to vanity, ego and the things of this world. Mainly, his high opinions of himself and his feeling that he has a firm grasp on reality and how to live his life in the best possible way."

"He has a choice but he fails to see that he has fallen in his imagination for the wrong choice, that of slavery to the lower powers around himself … the lower powers of the Kal, usually the astral influences and powers of the Kal and Brahm, although a few make it into the Mental Plane and are trapped within its lower forces of influence and limited states of consciousness."

"When a man is in a cave that is of total darkness and he ventures into a cave with a 3 foot hole in the ceiling that lets in the light of the sun, he may imagine that he has entered heaven itself."

"But then, if he climbs out of that hole in the cave into the forest where the sun shines and there are flowers and trees, he may think again that this is his true home heaven."

"This is what happens as man makes his way through the lower worlds of time and space. He moves from a lower state to a higher state and falsely believes he has found freedom, when in fact, he has only elevated his consciousness slightly when compared to the totality of life."

A.F. "This is all fascinating, but how does it tie into the use of imagination?"

R.T. "Good you have finally asked. I will continue."

"The first thing we need to understand is that with imagination, we need a target or object or objective on which to focus. Imagination is sort of like a search light of attention."

"See, it is really attention and focus we are after but imagination is actually a faculty operating within Soul. We sometimes call this the imaginative faculty."

"So what or who exactly do we direct our imagination and attention towards? Do we direct it towards the Kal power and his many lower streams of consciousness?"

"Do we direct it at the various lower powers or some sort of fatherly space God that will act as a Santa Claus and give us our wishes in the realms of time and space?"

"So we can have this space God manipulate our own reality, give us better health, a better job, a better home, human love and more money in our pockets."

"Is this how we direct the greatest force in the lower worlds towards temporal self-interest and temporal self-gain?"

"The secret is, if used properly, imagination can be used to bring us into the orbit of the Spiritual Travelers. It can bring us to the Golden Wisdom Temples where we may study with the VARDAN Masters and study the Shariyat-Ki-HURAY in its various volumes scattered throughout all the worlds."

"These books contain all combined Wisdom in the lower as

well as higher worlds and yet, few know of them and fewer, still, are aware of having studied them with a VARDAN Master and temple guardian."

"The truth learned in these Golden Wisdom Temples is like no other, because the truth that man learns is a lie."

"He is engaged in the illusions of the Kal. Man squanders away his time studying the countless sub-forces of the universe, but never does he realize that these sub-forces or energies will never give him Freedom, Love, Wisdom, nor Power; only pain and more incarnations in the lower worlds."

"To get above these lower forces one needs 5 things.

1. The Margatma, the Living VARDAN Master.

2. The spiritual exercises of VARDANKAR

3. The VARDAN Sound Current

4. The true initiation or link up with the Sound or Audible Life Stream through the perfect Master.

5. The HURAY or one true God."

"Of these five things, the perfect Master is the first that one must find. When I say perfect Master, I am not in any way, shape or form, referring to you in the physical plane. Oh no. As you are well aware in the physical, you are not perfect. Far from it."

AF: "Yes, I know."

Rebazar began to laugh.

RT: "Sometimes I think you do not believe you are truly the Master because of your outer imperfections but it is the inner that we seek, not the outer. The lower bodies must catch up with the inner. This is always the way it has been and will be. Take me for example. I am now over 550 years of age in the same body. Few believe this because I look in my 30's. Why? Because I am needed right now. It is not because I fear death!"

Rebazar laughed again. It was a deep laugh almost from his belly.

RT: "So I say this to you. Do not dismay if you are not perfect in the outer. In the outer, we do the best that we can. We can do no more than this. But what I am trying to convey today to everyone reading is a general understanding of how imagination is applied in your daily life."

"To apply the imagination to gain material wealth, success and happiness, as man defines happiness, is for the most part a waste of time. The laws of karma and the temporal nature of these lower worlds will see to it that man suffers in the end. This world is not Soul's true home and never will be."

"To apply the imagination to find God is the key. All other reasons need to remain subservient to this one true goal."

"If we are to become spiritually free, we must free our minds of limitation and dogma. Then we begin to see that we have imprisoned ourselves as Soul in that dark dingy prison some call the human skull!"

"As long as Soul is trapped in the body, it can never be free."

"Yes, a man may die. He may be murdered, have an accident or die of some disease or even old age. Although he will go into another world, he will find himself back on Earth soon enough to face another lifetime."

"This will go on and on and on for him. And as long as he remains in the body consciousness, he will not be free; although he may beg for forgiveness from God, he does not understand that he is praying to the Kal Niranjan, the king of the lower worlds and the Kal's job is to keep Soul trapped in these lower worlds."

"It is true man may find himself temporarily in the astral world and it can certainly be nicer in certain parts of the Astral than in the physical Earth world. For some, this is all they want. But it is a world of illusion and death. They may dwell in the Astral World for 10 years or 10,000 years but, sooner or later they will leave for the astral body will die, or they will be called back for more schooling on Earth or one of the other planets occupying the Pinda or Physical Plane of existence."

"If man wants freedom, he must study the works of VARDANKAR and enroll as a member and after two years become an initiate. He must put his heart into his study and engage in true contemplation upon the VARDAN works."

"Then and only then, will he have a goal or vision to which he may turn his powerful imaginative faculty towards!"

"If he turns his imagination toward the temporal goals of this world he shall only in the end find pain and suffering on the 'wheel of 84' or life and death in the form of almost countless lifetimes."

"When we put spiritual freedom off for another lifetime, we never really know how long it will be till we are given another chance to meet the Master and return back to the HURAY."

"It may be in the next life or it may be 100,000 years from

now, or a million lifetimes."

"Only the spiritual traveler can say."

"Some turn their divine imagination towards helping their fellow man. This is a kalistic goal."

"What man is saying is, he shall not return back to God nor find enlightenment but, instead, help with the management of the lower worlds. This is in the domain of the Kal and this man, although he may be admired, is only doing the Kal's work of keeping Souls in these worlds through false promises that this world is Soul's true home and that Souls should remain here and worship the Kal or Brahm as God, instead of finding the Spiritual Traveler and returning to HURAY within this lifetime or the next."

"When one uses imagination or the imaginative faculty, certain principles will make it far easier."

"There are several I will cover here."

"Firstly, a childlike attitude of expectancy is very important. Remember the attitude of a child who expects a bicycle for Christmas and is anticipating it. He knows it will be there on that day and has full faith in his father."

"There is a childlike joy and innocence, an enthusiasm and a total lack of apathy or negativity. Children very naturally have this positive expectancy and trust in the great spirit of life."

"It is generally only after the parents of teachers get a hold of a child, is there a danger of this changing, or if the child has had a violent past life that has carried through."

"But a happy well-adjusted young child, say of the age of

between 2 and 4, will have this very trusting joyful approach to life, this childlike trust."

"The child also has little, if any dogma programmed into him or her, so there is little of that skepticism or beliefs that things are impossible."

"Have you ever listened to a very young child talk about life? They, perhaps, want to become an Astronaut and visit other planets where there is life. Or be a Baseball player."

"The adults often chuckle to themselves and think how naive the child is. If they only knew that NASA does not except many Astronauts or that the space shuttle only orbits the Earth."

"They think the child is being naive but fortunately they usually go along with him and allow him his foolish dreams."

"Later in life, they will try and convince him to set his sights much lower, perhaps a Farmer or Pharmacist? A Dentist or even an Auto Mechanic or Factory Worker?"

"As far as the silly idea of the Astronaut or Baseball Player; well it was cute when they were 4, but now that they're 13, it's time to get real!"

"This attitude has also been transposed into the spiritual. Man does not believe that he can go to heaven until after his death. He does not believe man can find God in this lifetime. He does not believe much of anything, other them some stodgy old book and a bunch of superstition and dogma about various men who were somehow different than him in some mysterious way. These men, of course, died long ago and no one can speak with them except, perhaps, some intermediator such as a Priest or Psychic."

"This is the worst sort of use of imagination. If I tell a child that he is trapped inside his body, perhaps I don't tell him that directly, but I imply it and teach him dogma and superstition."

"Man is sick. He is lacking in truth and his ignorance is appalling. VARDANKAR often elicits a very negative reaction from some because it flies in the face of their cherished beliefs. Mainly that life is of a materialistic and emotional nature and that somehow God will reward us if we are good and follow our religion."

"There are countless different belief systems as you know."

"Some call themselves humanists and believe that there is no God and that man must worship being a good human being and doing good things. That this is all there is to life."

"I will not cover all the varied beliefs that people have. There are so many that I would say everyone in the end has a different belief than the next, although some are more closely aligned than others."

"This is not the point that I can name all the different millions of belief systems for you. The real point is actually quite simple; that each of these beliefs and states of consciousness have one thing in common ... that of imagination."

"They become real in the imaginations of those who subscribe to them and participate in them."

"They are all states of consciousness and are closely tied with the imaginative faculty of man."

"If you can control someone's imagination, you can control him. This has been used by tyrants and religious leaders alike."

"This is because as many have pointed out man has trouble telling the difference between reality and imagination."

"It is not until Soul goes into the Higher Worlds above the Etheric or subconscious part of the Mental Plane and reaches the Atma or Soul plane, also known as the 5th plane, that he finds the first of the true Pure Positive God Worlds of VARDAN."

"In this world of the ATMA Lok, Soul knows through direct perception. The mind is dropped and Soul exists in this world of Seeing, Knowing and Being!"

"In order to reach this first of the Pure Positive God Worlds, Soul generally needs the aid of a true Spiritual Traveler."

"Few reach this level without their help. I have to say there is a vast world of darkness and energy right before one reaches the Soul plane or ATMA Lok that appears impenetrable and made of nothingness. This many call the void. There are several voids dividing each plane, but the void between the Soul plane and etheric is particularly difficult to transverse and the few who make it this far generally, will falsely conclude that God is nothing! And they have reached enlightenment and found this dark vast field of nothing filled with energy."

"There is a false feeling that one is being absorbed into the universe and that one cannot go any further and they have reached the ultimate state of awareness."

"This is, of course, not true at all. They have not even made it into the ATMA Lok, let alone reached the Anami or 10th plane or the beginnings of true God Realization!"

"The imagination must be worked through the presence of

the Living VARDAN Master."

"The Inner Master is always with his chelas. He is closer than their heartbeat. The chela must learn to become aware of this presence. Then he will begin to make proper use of his imagination in order to break free of the lower worlds and find self and God Realization in this lifetime."

"The chela must learn to die daily. He leaves his body during his spiritual exercises while his body is safely watched by a Spiritual Traveler. Then he returns to his body born anew."

"This has always been the way back to God and nothing else but this will do."

"The imagination of man has been used mostly to enslave him inside his own skull and cause him great fear and hardship ... or generate for him temporarily material success, wealth and temporal material and emotional happiness."

"But this false happiness was emotional in nature and quickly turned to pain as pleasure and pain are simply two sides of the same problem of countless incarnations in the lower worlds."

"Man must now make a decision. Do I use my imagination to visualize a world brought about by the Kal in order to enslave me and give me a false sense of freedom? Or do I abandon all pretense and dogma and follow the Margatma into the splendid worlds of light and sound above illusion."

"In order to do the latter, we must learn the proper use of imagination."

"I will cover this topic in more detail later on."

"That is all for now!"

20

PART TWO ON IMAGINATION

RT: "Now, Allen, I wish to cover Divine Imagination in greater detail. How does one keep one's attention on Soul and the Master and upon God? This is actually quite simple."

"Remember the discourse where we talked about Sound; light and sound and how it emanates from the Godhead and issues down into the lower worlds, where it hits bottom then returns back to ITS source?"

"Well, this is a part of the key to Divine Imagination. But there is a problem. At first we cannot focus on this light and sound because of the nature of the lower worlds and the various lower barriers that separate Soul from truth through the lower nature of man. So instead we must place our attention upon the perfect Master, the Living VARDAN Master. Not the outer Master, but the Inner Master, who is the personification or personalization of that which is impersonal."

"This allows the human state of being to free itself from the enslavement of the Kal Niranjan or king of the negative worlds."

"So we place our imaginations upon that which is pure: the face of the Living VARDAN Master and on God."

"When we do this, we begin to exclude all that is unpure from our world. We are dealing with not only divine imagination here, but with the Living VARDAN Master and with truth ITSELF!"

"Since the Living VARDAN Master always dwells in the Higher Worlds and is, in reality the VARDAN of ITSELF in an embodiment of the many lower bodies, we can grab a hold of this matrix or power structure and within it, connect with that which is indestructible, perfect and pure: the VARDAN stream and ultimately the Anami Lok and above."

"If man were to try and do this without the Living VARDAN Master, it would be so beyond his keen of imagination that it would be virtually useless."

"Therefore, man uses the matrix or form of the outer Master to reach the perfect form of the Inner Master and from there the Inner Master, being the VARDAN of ITSELF, acts as a pure channel or funnel to bring the chela into the awareness of the ecstatic states of beingness."

"Mainly, Seeing, Knowing and Being through direct perception and this, my friend, is the rub as they say in the Earth world."

"Man cannot find God any other way because God is simply too far above man's perceptions. Most men are so caught up in the hard Physical, Astral and Mental Worlds that, there is little room for anything else. This is why most pray to a space God, in a vain attempt for man to find the things and comforts of this world."

"Man pretends that this is spiritual in nature. The seeking of God to fulfill his heart's desires. But in reality, man is an utter materialist! His only desire is for emotional comforts and physical sex, food, and gold."

"He desires human love and sex, friendship and feelings of happiness and bliss of a material nature. But in the end all he gets is pain and more incarnations."

"Man is a fool trying to bargain with a false God for his happiness through material salvation. Man seeks material and emotional salvation which does not exist."

"The emotions and physical body of man will never bring him happiness nor joy for long. It is an illusion or mirage."

"The space Gods that man prays to give him nothing in return for his devotion, except pain and suffering on the long 'wheel of 84' where he must endure millions upon millions of incarnations."

"Man is a fool. His ideas and ideals of mental, emotional and physical perfection are false. Man shall never reach perfection in the lower bodies although he may try."

"And if man were sincere, he would cease to focus on this negative world and give his love and devotion to the HURAY or one true God above all matter, energy, space and time."

"But man, in a vain attempt to live forever in the ego consciousness, does not seek God; only the things of this world and the lower worlds of the Astral, Causal and perhaps, Mental Plane."

"That is all man knows therefore he is, in effect, blind and deaf to the Living VARDAN Master, who attempts to give out truth to the ignorant masses of people who, quite frankly, do not want it."

"They only desire materialism at its worst and most base level: that of saving bodies, maintaining bodies, helping bodies and managing the lower forces of nature, to gain some imaginary benefits of an emotional, mental or physical nature."

"Man does not realize that his is the improper use of Divine Imagination. Man is like the fool wasting his gold pieces on wine, women and song. Soon, man will realize that all of his suffering is in vain and that all this time he could have had God, if he had only been sincere and spent his good karma on finding the Living VARDAN Master and gaining enlightenment through Out-of-Body Tuza or Soul Travel.

"The golden coins of divine imagination really consist of three things."

1. Love and devotion.
2. Attention
3. Dedication to that which is eternal.

"We can also add a fourth which is selflessness."

"Of these, the first two are most important. But the question begs asking. What do we give our love and devotion to? Surely not the helping of physical and astral bodies or the acquiring of wealth and power? What must we give our love and devotion to?"

"Why God and the Master of course! Are you beginning to see? For what we give our love and devotion too is what we shall have. If we give our love and devotion to the acquisition of gold, then it might take 10 years or it might take 10 lifetimes, but eventually we shall have gold. It is a fact that what a Soul places its attention and love upon lay manifest unto it and that nothing, not even Heaven and Earth, can stop this in the long run. In the short run yes, but in the long run if a Soul uses love, devotion and attention, they will gain the object of their devotion."

"But, of course, this must be paid for in some form or coin."

"Therefore, if a man desires a million dollars in gold, he may have that for which he seeks but at what price?"

"What good is it for a man to gain all the gold in the universe and lose his Soul?

"No Good!

"No God!!!"

Rebazar laughed.

R.T.: "I cannot tell you exactly how many individuals get lost in their love and devotion to self, or more accurately, their little self.

"It seems to be a disease in this world."

"Anyway, continuing on, if our love and devotion is misplaced, then we shall not just eventually get what we place our attention upon, but we shall pay for this in some manner."

"This is a spiritual law in this world."

"When one generates good karma, it's simply cause and effect. If one uses their good karma to acquire the things of this world and not the opportunity to find the Margatma, the Living

VARDAN Master, then all is lost and that person is, in a way, squandering their good karma for the things of this world. For things like human love, sex, admiration, devotion to personalities, embodiments, social approval, wealth, power, rich foods and fine clothing, intellectual superiority, emotional superiority, perhaps even psychic powers of perception, such as telepathic powers, telekinesis, seeing into the past and future and so forth."

"Man may learn to appear in the dream states of others, but this is generally wrong unless he is given permission."

"The point being made here is that without proper focus, man wanders around and around on the 'wheel of 84' trying to find himself through the things of this world and the lower worlds, but only finds emptiness."

"If man uses his imagination for this, then he is not only wasting it but often creating more karma; for he will be tempted to misuse these forces of the Kal for his own selfish pleasures and self-aggrandizement."

"The true devotee of the Master and God understands that the little self must give way to the greater self. That Soul must be in the driver's seat, and the only honest way of achieving this is through Out-of-Body Tuza Travel with the help of the Master."

"If a man were to only reach the Astral regions, he has not found truth nor has he found anything of lasting value."

"If a man goes into the Causal or Mental Plane instead, he is little better off than the first man who has reached astral awareness or realization."

"If a man somehow manages to reach the high mind or

Etheric Plane, although he may by now have enormous psychic powers, he has not reached anything of truly lasting or eternal nature but only reached the high mind; but falsely thinks he has given up the ego and is pure Soul."

"He is not pure Soul and as such, is still in a world of illusion. Until he moves past the great void or area of darkness that separates the lower worlds from the higher worlds, he is only operating in the field of opposites, mountains and valleys, love and hate."

"The Etheric Plane may give the illusion that is it beyond opposites but, this is only because it is the last frontier before Soul finds itself in the world of Sat Nam, who is the ruler on the Soul Plane or what is known in VARDANKAR as the Atma Lok. Sat Nam is the first true manifestation of the HURAY and at this point, Soul knows through direct perception all things and yet, Soul is still a far cry from perfection, having only found true Self Realization but not God realization.

"The idea that when one knows their little self: their body, emotions and mind, they are self-realized is a falsehood. It is simply not true. How could a man understand life through the eyes of the Kal or negative power?"

"One cannot. He must see life from the viewpoint of Soul and in order to do this, man must learn Out-of-Body Tuza Travel with the Living VARDAN Master of his times."

"If a man goes to the Astral World, he is not going to find truth. If he goes further than this, still nothing but the true Pure Positive God Worlds will yield him the true realizations and eternal consciousness that the true God seeker seeks within his lifetime."

"There will be those who will accuse the VARDANIST of escapism. Of trying to avoid life by traveling into these other worlds. This is not true. The VARDANIST is not into escapism but is, in reality, the most responsible of all men for he or she understands that before one can help his fellow man, he must help himself. From the VARDAN streams all true Love, Wisdom, Power, Freedom and even beyond this.

"Therefore, if one desires to be useful to God, he must seek God not in the lower worlds of time or space, but where God dwells in the Higher Worlds. Then man may serve God as a conscious co-worker and not serve the Kal Niranjan in the management of lower bodies and karmic debts.

"So perhaps you see that divine imagination is best used to find God and not to find materiality?"

"When one loves something, they spend time in the absorption and vibratory field of that which they love and are devoted too."

"If a lover truly loves his beloved, does he not desire to spend much time with his beloved? If a true God seeker truly desires God and truth, then does he or she not desire to spend as much time as possible with God and with Truth?"

"How can one put their imagination upon something they are not near? Therefore, we must submerge ourselves in Truth."

"We must study the VARDAN works. We must practice the spiritual exercises as laid down by the Living VARDAN Master in the discourses, talks and books."

"We must become a magnet of truth by magnetizing our heart with love and devotion and studying the words and clever techniques of the Living VARDAN Master."

"Then we begin to become absorbed in truth and we have a way of bringing our divine imagination in to the orbit of truth through our own attention, devotion and love for truth."

"If we keep a distance from truth, we shall not find it. When one keeps their distance, they are not inside of the magnetic field of that which they are trying to avoid."

"In a sense, they become an outsider to that which they view from afar. You cannot know something by keeping far away. You must get closer and finally, when you have decided that this is what you desire, you must get still closer and closer until you and the object of your interest are so close, in fact, that you have an intimate relationship with it."

"This is true of all things in this world and frankly in a sense, also true of the other worlds above this one."

"We do not have to gain this intimacy all at once. We may use caution if we choose to. We may approach slowly and surely but, at some point, if we stop getting closer to the object we are approaching, then our progress stops at that point and will generally go no further."

"This is precisely the problem with many. They have a standoffishness to life, to God, to truth, to the Master; and for this they pay the price of feeling a lack of spiritual progress due to their holding back. What they are doing, in fact, is holding truth at bay!"

"We must, if we desire truth, always move forward toward truth. If we stop for whatever reason and discontinue our desire and movement towards truth and towards God, then there will be a heavy price to pay. The price being that we will fail to find God and fail to find truth."

"Those that say finding truth is impossible are foolish. These people do not desire truth for themselves nor for anyone else. It is the height of arrogance to think that truth cannot be found. IT CAN. But one must be humble before God and the Master and stop trying to make truth fit into their own preconceived notions and expectations."

"Dogma is not truth; only dogma.

"Frankly, most men are frightened of truth and frightened of God!

"This is why man has tried, through religion, to make God in his own image. Do you notice this? God has a deep booming voice and wares a white robe? He, in masculine form, is often thought of as a father figure. He or God is strong, powerful, protecting of "his children." This is man attempting to define God as a person. Albeit, a person with great powers!

"And what powers does man try and give his space gods or false God's? Read the bible or other so called holy books from the various man made religions and you will see that, God helps man win wars, defeat his enemies in battle, feed the masses, heal the sick, bear children, find gold and so forth and so on.

"Even in heaven, man has made God materialistic. Man imagines banquet tables where he may sit by the side of God, who appears as a mighty man and dine with God!"

"Why does man try and reduce God to a mere image of a human being? Because man is afraid of God, therefore, he tries to chain his God up and make him mortal!"

"Think about this! Man has created a God who is more powerful than he is, but not so much more powerful than him, that he can't understand God."

"Man desires to break everything into the most base of desires. Look in the Christian bible again and you will see references in the Old Testament to God being angry and jealous. That God wants people to worship him. That God is a jealous God and wants admiration, love, devotion and sacrifices."

"Does this sound like the HURAY, the one true God beyond time, and space, beyond duality? NO I say, it sounds more like some powerful King who is selfish and is looking out for his own self-interests and wants to be worshiped in personality form."

"This is not God but only a reflection of the lower lords of the lower worlds of time and space."

"This is man reducing his God to that of a superman with super powers that serve him and aid in his life. Man wants a god that will serve him, while he pretends that he will serve God."

"Even the so called selfless people really, for the most part, do not desire God; they only desire to feel happiness, love, bliss and good about themselves and their life."

"There is nothing wrong with this but it is NOT the desire for God that they are after; only the imagined benefits that they want to receive from their imaginary God."

"The Brahm and Kal serve man by delaying his journey to the true God HURAY. And man falls for this hook, line and sinker."

"Man uses his imagination to create all kinds of fake and false realities and illusions because man, frankly, does not want truth; he only wants the comforts of this world and the social order of things."

"He wants devoted friends and family who love him dearly; he wants to be admired by his peers and loved ones alike. He wants to feel important and accomplished in many areas of his life. He wants to feel powerful, loved, accomplished, confident, loving, just, admired, respected, revered, celebrated, welcomed, rich, and so forth. He thinks that God will give him all of these things, so he tells his God that if his God will give him all of this, he will serve his God in turn. But man does not want to serve God; only to serve himself and man, quite frankly, is lying to himself on this. He has fooled himself into thinking he desires to serve his God when, in reality, he desires his God to serve him! He has lied to himself and said he desires to serve his fellow man when, in fact, he really desires his fellow man to serve him."

"All of this mess is of the Kal or negative power; as long as man does not learn Out-of-Body Tuza travel and learn to transcend the lower worlds of opposites, he will suffer from illusion and delusion."

"The spiritual travelers or VARDAN Masters offer man hope, but most men spit in their faces, or worse, for they don't want truth. They don't even want God nor the true eternal bliss of God. They only want the things of this world."

"To them, if heaven does not contain the five passions and all the things they love such as sex, human love, vanity, devotion, emotionalism, fine sensations of taste and smell, visual beauty and fine music, thoughts, ideas and images that strike cords of happiness, and on, and on and on; then they really want no part of heaven at all. Their imaginations are so underdeveloped that, they cannot imagine a life without the Kal or negative qualities. They have, in their own imaginations, turned heaven into Earth and Earth into heaven."

"The entire world is turned upside down and what is good becomes evil and what is evil becomes good."

"As I have said, evil is anything that delays Soul from returning to God and good is anything that helps Soul return back to God faster. But the average man would violently disagree with this statement since he does not truly want to return to God, but only to his primitive state or animalistic state."

"There are those who worship this animalistic side of man and even give blood sacrifices unto their false Gods. Even in the Christian religion, they speak of Jesus being nailed to a cross and sacrificing himself in order to absorb man's sins."

"How does this differ from the blood sacrifices of the ancient cultures of the Aztecs or Mayans where a virgin was murdered?"

"There is little or no difference, except man has sanctioned this as something holy and spiritual. It makes no sense why God would care if we took a man or an animal and murdered it and then declared that this animal or man has died, in order to save us from our own self."

"The Christians will argue that Jesus was the only begotten son of God, therefore because he was so special, this explains why he could die and absolve us from all responsibility for our own conduct and let us go to heaven, despite little or no effort on our part."

"This is a religion for the lazy where a man can do whatever he pleases and then at the last minute say, he accepts Jesus and goes to heaven."

"It is not heaven where he goes to but, perhaps if he is lucky, he will spend some time in the low to mid astral regions, but that is about all he can expect for having such foolish beliefs."

"But again, this serves man's desire to bring God down to his level. That God actually would be moved by the death of a human body and forgive everyone on Earth for all eternity because of it, only makes sense if you are of a very base and primitive viewpoint of seeing God as a man or King, who has his own foolish whims and desires, but is very powerful and may grant certain wishes if you can gain his favor."

"The HURAY, on the other hand, is not moved by any of this false drama. IT does not care about embodiments, but only of Soul returning to IT in ITS humble abode in the Ocean of Love and Mercy."

"So, perhaps, you see that the imagination is like a fine steel sword, so sharp as to be dangerous and yet, so sharp as to be Soul's salvation if Soul can use it in the right way."

"And what is this "right way?" Simply the way of VARDANKAR, the Ancient Science of Out-of-Body Tuza or Soul travel. Out-of-body Tuza Travel has no limitations in this world or any other world, for that matter. It is not limited to the mere Astral Plane nor the Causal, Mental or Etheric Planes of the lower worlds of M.E.S.T. (matter, energy, space and time).

"It is not limited in any way, for this is the great secret that the Kal or negative power does not want man to know: that salvation is here and now. That God is here and now! And all Love, Wisdom, Power and Freedom is here and now!

"That Soul may leave its lower bodies and travel by the side of the great Spiritual Travelers, the VARDAN Masters, and leave these lower worlds and see the real face of God or HURAY.

"IT is not a human face, but must be experienced and until it is, nothing can be said about IT.

"This is the journey ... the great adventure. And the imaginative faculty is a vital tool that Soul uses in its arsenal, to find spiritual freedom in the here and now. Within this lifetime, and not having to wait for the next or listen to the false promises of the Kal of finding truth at some later date that never comes.

"Man can have truth, but he must want truth and not be so self-deluded as to put God into some human form, or see his base human desires as his ultimate goals."

And with that, the Great VARDAN Master, Rebazar Tarzs ended his sermon and disappeared into the mountains. I think he had sensed I was tired of writing and needed to rest.

21

SURRENDER TO THE MASTER

It was morning and Rebazar seemed eager to get started.

RT: "Today, as you know, we are going to cover Surrender to the Master. Now you don't entirely understand this, so I am going to go slowly and advance accordingly."

"Man has always had a problem with his ego. When I say "always" I am, of course, speaking of that day he descended into the lower worlds and took on his various lower bodies, for the purpose of enlightenment or, I should say, true enlightenment which is the consciousness and realization found on first the Atma Lok or Soul Plane, where man finds Self Realization and secondly, God Realization found from the Anami Lok upwards."

"Man seems to be in direct opposition to this world and all its dealings. He struggles against the very spiritual laws that bind him to this world...for most so-called spiritual laws are really simply lower manifestations of the Kal Niranjan or negative power."

"The only true spiritual law is the law of love, but that's an entirely different subject."

"Moving on, we see that man cannot be a greater channel

than his own self-limiting consciousness, so when we desire to be a channel for the God power or we desire to have this God power flow through us as vehicles for IT, then we must learn surrender."

"This is why so few make it into the God worlds and only manage to reach the psychic regions of the Astral, Causal and Mental Planes respectively."

"They have failed to surrender to the Master, therefore their mind and emotions entrap them."

"Even if they were to somehow perfect these to some high degree, they are still nonetheless trapped, for the Kal power has clever ways of trapping those Souls who fail to venture into the Higher Worlds with the Living VARDAN Master, or one of his appointees or one of the other great VARDAN Masters, such as myself, Yaubl Sacabi, or many others too numerous to mention here."

"There is a vast spiritual network of true God beings who help man evolve. This is not to be confused with the lower masters, who are masters of the lower planes such as the Astral or Casual. These are not true spiritual Masters but only teachers. Some teach Souls well while others do not."

"It does not matter for, when a Soul finally manages to find the Living VARDAN Master, they should cease to place their attention upon other so called masters and place it squarely upon the VARDAN teachings and the unifying factor of Out-of-Body Tuza Travel, via the Audible Life Stream through the body of the Margatma or Margatma Consciousness."

"This Margatma Consciousness permeates all things and yet, it is not all things. It is that presence that exists beyond time and space. One could say it is the highest state of consciousness and allows the presence of the HURAY on this Earth world with each Soul, who agrees to surrender to IT and the Master."

"Just as a body needs a liver in order to survive, we need the Master in order to find truth much like a child needs its mother, until he is of age where he can take care of himself."

"No truly loving mother wants her son to be dependent on her when he is of age, but she wants him to grow up to be a capable adult who can stand on his own two feet."

"This is also true of the Margatma, the Living VARDAN Master. He desires his chelas to stand on their own feet spiritually and eventually when qualified, reach spiritual mastership."

"But for this to happen, has little or nothing to do with any mental understanding nor emotional self-control, nor any of the orthodox methods as taught by the metaphysicians, philosophers or religionists. VARDANKAR is not about memorizing books or passages, nor parroting the words of the Master. None of this will bring one into the heart of God or HURAY."

"What we are after is nothing less than the experience of God Realization and for this to occur, we need to learn to surrender to the Inner Master and turn over our burden to him and follow him into the shining worlds beyond the Soul plane into the Anami Lok, where the light and sound are indescribable and Soul finds eternal ecstasy."

"When one partakes of these high, high, worlds, they become like a fountain of light and sound, which contains the sum total of all known Love, Wisdom, Power and Freedom."

"They become a light unto this world. That is, if they have

surrendered to this power, this consciousness and not simply passively witnessed its splendor."

"Even then, they are changed beings forever. One cannot begin this journey expecting any physical reward whatsoever."

"The Kal will see to it that one suffers, for to bring the light and sound of the higher worlds into this world of darkness is to confront the Kal Niranjan, one's Achilles heel. That of the Audible Life Stream that brings Soul back home to God."

"When one is a channel for this Audible Life Stream, they will be under almost constant attack from the agents of the Kal and they must choose to serve the HURAY without any thought of reward or face the wrath of the lower worlds. In other words, one cannot split sides. You are either on the side of the Kal or the VARDAN. To try and do both is like the fool who tries to ride two horses at the same time, putting his right leg on the white one and his left leg on the brown one. When the two horses split up, one leg must either let go or there will be much pain and suffering."

"And this pain and suffering brings me to the topic at hand, that of surrender."

"When one cries out for God and desires nothing but God, then he will be given the opportunity to surrender."

"First, he learns of the teachings of VARDANKAR and must study them if he is to find spiritual liberation and then God Realization."

"Once he has decided if they are right for him, generally after two years of study, he may ask for his second initiation."

"Then he works out all his earthly karma and does not have

to incarnate on the Earth. This continues through each corresponding initiation. The initiations are a link up with the VARDAN Stream or Audible Life Current. This is the force, as I have said countless times, that sustains all of life and returns to God. Soul may ride this light and sound with the help of the Master back into the very heart of God...but this is generally done slowly in order to preserve the body and keep the lower bodies balanced."

"If the Master were to take his student into the Anami Lok right away, they would most likely become unbalanced and have great spiritual troubles and difficulties that might overwhelm them, and render them useless to God, their family and to themselves."

"Therefore, the Master not only acts as a way shower but regulates the pace of the chela, so that he does not go too far out of balance. This is why some move faster along the path than others."

"It's simply some are more ready, but all are loved by the Master. It is the nature of the VARDAN or divine spirit to love all Souls for Soul is composed of the VARDAN ITSELF. Soul is the eternal individualization of the VARDAN and as such, perceives through direct perception, seeing, knowing and being. Soul has a 360 degree viewpoint and can operate without a mind in the higher worlds, but needs a mind in order to interact in the lower worlds, much like a deep sea diver needs a diving suit to interact at 1000 feet below."

"Many foolishly think they can reach God without the Spiritual Traveler. But this is vanity at its worst."

"Yes, it is true that most, if not all so called masters are not true Masters, but false masters who are doing things for their own egos and benefit. This has tainted a lot of people and caused them to rebel against the whole idea of finding a Master."

"They now want to study many paths at the same time and try and follow many teachings, saying that they are all the same. That everyone knows truth. That truth is accessible to the masses through certain books and all they have to do is combine different paths and teachings into a hodge-podge and they can then find God."

"This is the worst kind of insanity and these people suffer greatly or they are simply fools pretending to desire God but only talk, and talk, and talk never leaving their bodies; or if so, only into the lower worlds: generally the astral world and not even the High Astral."

"No one would try and learn the violin from a book. If they had any desire to be a great violinist, they would require an extremely competent music teacher and virtuoso to teach them."

"And yet, finding God is almost infinitely more difficult than learning to play a musical instrument, and yet these fools fail to realize that and arrogantly go off in their own direction without a Master."

"Now here is a secret that most do not know or desire to talk about. Even when the chela or aspirant finds the Margatma, the Living VARDAN Master and surrenders to him; this is not enough, because what the chela thinks of as surrender is generally completely separate from the truth."

"This is a precious secret I shall share with you on this morning."

"What man tries to surrender, is his little self or, more

accurately, parts of his little self. But he generally refuses to surrender his real self to the Master, of course, his real self being his true eternal essence Soul or his God self."

"The chela will surrender those parts of himself, such as certain parts of his personality that he no longer thinks he wants or needs. This is something, quite frankly, the Master does not really want. But the Master will thank the chela for surrendering these unwanted parts and dispose of them in the VARDAN stream, much like taking out the trash!"

"See this is funny!" Rebazar Tarzs grinned."

RT: "The Master is only interested in Soul and not in the lower bodies and yet, the chela thinks that the Master wants his lower attributes. So the chela may surrender say, his anger on a certain issue and say: Here Master, I surrender myself to you. But in reality, the chela is only surrendering a part of his anger."

"And the Master will take this part of the lower self and accept it and pass it into the VARDAN stream. And the chela actually thinks he is making progress and surrendering to the Master. And, in a way, he is making progress but he has not surrendered to the Master; he has only discarded some garbage that he does not think he needs anymore."

"This will go on and on and on. Sometimes for years or even decades or centuries or longer!"

"So when the Master asks the chela to surrender and the chela starts giving up those lower parts of his lower bodies, the Master will not generally complain, because the Master knows that the chela needs to discard this junk in order to reach the next level. So the Master will generally thank him for doing this and the chela will often falsely believe that he has surrendered to the Master, when he has only given the Master some garbage to throw into the VARDAN stream."

"Now the chela might be able to learn to discard this psychic trash himself, but often it's far easier if he surrenders this burden or burdens to the Master. That is what this really is. It's a burden that the chela or student has been carrying around. Sometimes, for thousands or even millions of years!"

"So this is a good thing but it's not the kind of surrender that we are seeking. It is a lower form of surrender, but it does not lead to Self-Realization nor God-Realization."

"And there are many who do not understand this. I would say very few understand what the Shariyat-Ki-HURAY is talking about when it speaks of surrender to the Master."

"What God and the Master desire, is that Soul surrenders ITSELF to the Inner Master. Soul is all the Master is really interested in. Not the lower bodies."

"What we have here is a sort of shell game taking place. You know a shell game where someone hides a little ball under one of three cups? It's an optical illusion, a trick."

"Because the hand is quicker than the eye, the shell game can be used to fool people into believing something is true when, in fact, it is not. The ball may be nowhere to be found, or it may be in an entirely different cup than it appears."

"The lower self, consisting of the lower bodies and karma of man is not his true Self. This false self, little self or ego self is a projection of reality, much like a TV projection set or movie projector projects a false image onto a flat screen."

"This illusion of self consists of many parts too numerous to mention, but I will try. We have various levels of the mind and emotional or astral body. We have the entire physical body, it's brain and autonomic nervous system and the various organs such as the heart, that carry sensations across the body."

"Did you know, for instance, that there is a tiny brain inside the heart? And this tiny brain communicates with our brain in our head. So when they say follow your heart, there is some scientific backing to this statement, although science is a sham for it fails to explain much of anything in this world."

"There are memories and images, also known as engrams or holographic projections from our almost countless experiences in life, going back into our past lives."

"Every time a drama or any sort of experience happens to us, it often forms these mental matrixes or picture files that contain energy."

"If, for example, you were murdered by being hung in a past life, you may get a sensation of tightness around the neck and not know why?"

"It is, often, simply this energy or picture file acting up for some odd reason. This, again, has nothing to do with our true self. It is a part of the causal body and not us."

"This association brings much pain; Soul associates or identifies with all sorts of things that, frankly, have nothing to do with Soul. They are necessary and mechanical in nature and they're simply lower bodies and the various parts and sub-energies that are needed, to make up the lower bodies of man."

"Take the human body which is the simplest of all of man's bodies and yet, it contains the microcosm of all the universes of universes at the cosmic consciousness level."

"Each electron and proton and sub-atomic particle spinning, mimics that of the various planets and galaxies. We, at the physical level, are a myriad of complexities and it's amusing to see how arrogant Medical Doctors, think they understand the human body when, in fact, they have absolutely no idea how it works or even what it is. It is, of course, made out of energy and a small quantity of matter. Mostly, it is a product of the universal mind power mixed with matter, in order to bring it into the density required for the physical universe, in order to exist here in this Earth world! In other words, it is an illusion!"

"So, we have the chela surrendering these illusions to the Master! But where is the chela in all of this? Oh where oh where could the chela be! Oh where oh where could he be!!!"

Rebazar laughed.

R.T. "You see, he is not really present. And this here lies the problem. The chela is so busy trying to sort through his lower world experiences that, he never thinks that maybe he is not really in them!"

"That there is a sort of dream and he is in a sort of dream-like state and that the reality is not found here, but in the Higher Worlds if he would just wake up."

"This is why the Master speaks of dying daily. That the chela must die daily. Then he finds he is dead to this world but alive. He is more alive than he could have ever possibly imagined, because he has found his true self! And not this false self that is posing or an imposter."

"So when the Master speaks of self-surrender, he is not really speaking of the lower self surrendering to him, but of the higher self. But he will not complain, for he knows that the chela needs to get this garbage out of him."

"If the chela truly understood what was happening, then he might discard the whole bin of trash all at once and simultaneously surrender his true God self onto the Master."

"But this is almost never done and for good reason."

"Firstly, few have the ability to do this. Secondly, the change in consciousness might shock the body into a bad state."

"We need these lower bodies in this world in order to interact with it. So if one were to do the above, it would send shock waves into the lower bodies that would disrupt their function and pull them way out of balance."

"It would, in essence, unhinge the individual and he would most likely be useless to society."

"He would have trouble integrating his experience and would, most likely, come unglued at the seams."

"Then it would be extremely difficult to go back into those higher states, because of the rubble that lay at his feet in his waking life."

"Some have tried this, but a true VARDAN Master will simply not allow a chela to do this, for the Master is responsible and will generally not take the chela out of his body into the Higher Worlds, until the time is right."

"This is why spiritual unfoldment must come naturally."

"Why the Master will not push one too fast or give them the inner realizations too quickly? To do so would be a disservice to the chela."

"There are, however, some in VARDANKAR who are ready Souls and have reached the higher initiations in past lives and have agreed, as Soul of course, to return here in service."

"Some of these Souls returned to this world out of choice, because of their great love for the HURAY and for their fellow Souls, who are suffering on the 'wheel of 84' through almost countless incarnations."

"Some have agreed to suffer at the hands of the Kal in order to free Souls and they have agreed to make faster spiritual progress and be pushed faster, in order to meet certain individual spiritual missions they have chosen and have been given to them."

"This is an act of Divine Love and some suffer because of it and are pushed along the path faster than might seem possible."

"You, in a way, were such a person and I know, at times, you don't feel qualified to carry on your job, but know this. That although challenging, I am watching and helping you whenever I can and there are others out there such as Yaubl, who are doing the same."

"We are all spiritual brothers and sisters and there is no competition, as you know; only the Law of Love."

AF: "Thank you, that means a lot. I have had much trouble with my health and emotions, and sometimes I feel I cannot go on but I must."

RT: "It will all make more sense later on but, know this. All Souls must grow and expand in consciousness. If it were too easy, then there would be little or no growth. This is why man fails to find the Master. They are looking for a certain pre-determined set of parameters or ideals that they have arbitrarily decided are necessary in order for one to be a true Master. When the Living VARDAN Master fails to meet their expectations and what they falsely believe to be their high standards, they discard him as worthless and look elsewhere."

"This is their right, but in the end they will fail to find a true VARDAN Master, because they are judging the Master through the eyes of the Kal or negative power, and are only looking for miracles and lower manifestations of truth; and not actually truth nor God, but the shadows and reflections of truth and of God."

"This is the point. True self surrender to the Master is the surrender of the true Self Soul. False self-surrender is the surrender of the false self."

"This is the same as the people who seek the false masters, because they desire something out of it. When one surrenders his psychic garbage, he is only giving the Master the things he no longer wants and is generally making a big deal over how willing he is to surrender when, in fact, he has not truly surrendered anything of value; only that which is an obstacle in his life."

"This may or may not help him on the path and often times, it does help for his burden becomes lighter and his attachment may be less severe. But until he surrenders his true self, he is really only wasting a lot of time and the Master will simply patiently wait and wait."

"Often, the chela will never get around to surrendering at all!!!" Rebazar laughed at this, as if thinking it was very funny."

RT: "Do you see the irony in this whole mess? The chela thinks he is surrendering to the Master and then he wonders why on Earth it's not working out the way he wishes. He thinks

234

that if he surrenders, all of heaven and Earth will be laid at his feet but this, generally, does not happen and he is disappointed. Then he might declare that the Master is a false Master. Perhaps this is best for all concerned because, quite frankly, the chela that does this lacks in sincerity."

"So, as always, it always goes back to the spiritual exercises as laid down by the Master and whether we are willing to die daily or not. If not, we are wasting our time in VARDANKAR and might just as well join some orthodox religion that does not require anything of us other than some money and the attendance of church services, on a weekly or monthly basis."

"Often, the chela will ponder the idea of surrender for years! I find this amusing, but normal. It does not mean the chela will fail. I have seen many VARDANISTS, such as yourself, stall and delay their surrender, and hem and haw and bring up all kinds of smoke screens, only to surrender at a later date."

"But I have seen many more who never seem to be able to surrender more than a few trash bags full of karma for the Master to discard."

"It is not that these students don't grow spiritually. I am not saying that at all; only that they will fail to reach their full spiritual potential, because of their unwillingness to surrender their true God self Soul to the Master. They, like I said, may offer all sorts of pseudo things to surrender to the Master, but he is really only interested in one thing. That he take that Soul into the heart of God where that Soul finds God Realization."

"To a lesser degree, he is interested in taking that Soul to the Soul plane to reach Self Realization. Even here, the Soul that surrenders to the Master, and I do mean truly surrenders and not just offers up his lower aspects, or his personality or phychic self, but surrenders his true self Soul to the Master, will find that the Master gives him all that he possesses."

"This is the amazing part of all of this. When the chela finally manages to truly surrender and give up all that he possesses, then the Master in turn gives the chela all that he possesses and then the God energy comes and draws the individual up through the returning Sound current into the high states of being and we have the realizations without all the resistance and pain, and barriers or filters that skew our view of truth. Unlike frosted glass or a dirty mirror, we may now enter into the full consciousness of the God worlds and reflect that light out into the world, as shining beacons of light and good will towards all Souls, who cry to return to God in the here and now."

"I have not said this right. It is difficult to form words on such lofty subjects. Words do not do any of this justice. How does one describe Soul in words, let alone the great HURAY? How does one describe the Master, the light giver to all the worlds?"

"How does one define the VARDAN, the Source of all that sustains all consciousness and is consciousness?

"I can only point the way, as you can only point the way. What Souls do with this information and the reading of this book is totally up to them. Many will accuse you of a gross imagination, and of being a profiteer or con man. Others may call you delusional or even psychotic.

"This is all to be expected. When one goes out on a limb, so to speak and brings the teachings public, they can expect to be attacked for their troubles. Most people do not want truth. They will fight truth at all cost and bitterly oppose it. To them I ask, why are you reading? Stop; you are wasting your time. Those who do not have the eyes to see nor the ears to hear shall never find truth. They are the blind and the deaf."

"To those who seek truth, I say truth will never be found in any book, nor talk, or lecture or discourse for that matter."

"All we can do. All that Allenji can do is show you the way and offer spiritual help upon the outer and inner planes."

"That is all. The rest is up to you. No true VARDAN Master cares whether you follow him or not. The choice is always up to you."

"This also holds true for surrender. The choice whether you desire to surrender your true God self Soul to the Master is totally an individual one."

"I can say no more than this."

"Goodbye for now. We shall talk again soon."

22

REBAZAR TARZS AND YAUBL SACABI
REVEAL THE SECRET OF SURRENDER

RT: "Now, my friend, I desire to reveal to you the secret of surrender. As we covered in the previous discourse yesterday morning, it is not about surrendering ones little self as most falsely imagine. Although the little self must be let go of, it is the Soul consciousness, our true God self that the Master desires and never the lower self. We can keep our lower bodies and our money, things and families. The Master really does not want any of this. It is of a lower nature and is useful in this world but not to God but to the Soul as an outward expression of the VARDAN in this world."

"But it is Soul our eternal self, as I explained in the last discourse that God desires to return to IT and take up Soul's rightful place within the spiritual hierarchy and become a conscious channel or vehicle for the God force in this world, as well as all worlds and universes upon universes."

"This is a tall order but one that Soul is destined to fulfill … but first, it must surrender itself to the Master. Not the outer Master but the Inner Master and to the HURAY and VARDAN of ITSELF."

"Now how does one go about this true self surrender? How does one surrender his true self and not his counterfeit self to the HURAY?"

"I will say this, my son."

"Imagine if you will the light and sound flowing through you. Of course, I am speaking of the returning wave. That wave that returns to the God force or HURAY and brings Soul back with it."

"This wave may rock soul, as if Soul is riding upon sunlit waves or crests of the great Ocean of Love and Mercy. Back and forth these waves vibrate as in a gentle rocking motion and the physical body and lower bodies may begin to rock back and forth in rhythm with this light and sound. This Audible Life Stream or current we call the VARDAN."

"The Master may call out to Soul to surrender to him and as Soul rocks back and forth upon this current, there is a gentle feeling of movement."

"But not yet I say, has Soul actually surrendered ITSELF to the Master or the VARDAN, let alone God."

"No not yet I say, but now we are close. As the sound continues to rock back and forth, there are two waves; one going outward sustaining all of life and creating all planes and manifestation, and then there is the far more important wave that moves Soul's back into the very heart of God."

"This rocking motion is yet caused by the play between these two waves: the outgoing wave and the returning wave."

"Out going, this wave sustains and creates all life. The returning wave brings Soul back into the center from where this mighty wave originated: the very heart of creation, the Ocean of Love and Mercy. The two waves are really one but they appear as separate waves until the full realization occurs on the 12th through 14th planes, even beyond the Anami Lok."

"As this rocking continues, as said before, Soul has still not surrendered to the Master but is getting closer."

"We now relax and trust the Master. We have gotten to this point because of our great love for God and our desire to return, but we still are not there yet. We are only on the cusp of success but not in its throes. There is still a part of us that is holding back, keeping ourselves separate from God, isolating our consciousness from that of the universal consciousness of the HURAY. Not the universal mind power, mind you, but the true higher consciousness of the Pure Positive God Worlds."

"We are nearing a form of insanity. Dancing on the edge of eternity but not there yet. In a state of limbo."

"But we must listen and still relax even more so. We must not stop this rocking motion nor this play, for as we rock between the inflow and outflow of the great cosmic sound current, we are like an automobile rocking back and forth trying to get out of a snow drift. As we rock back and forth in a gentle motion, the sound begins to take over our consciousness. At first, it becomes louder. The sound current may become overwhelming, the light may take on a brilliant white light of many suns and moons. We may see into the past, present and future and begin to feel the inner elation of the presence of the VARDAN. We are beginning to enter into the heart of life but are still standing strangely outside of it, as if we have one foot in heaven and the other in the spiritual material worlds and can't quite decide which we want to be a part of."

"This may go on but we must continue with this rocking motion and all the while, we must have an intense burning love for God and for the Master. This love is what draws us onto this ascending wave. We now may feel like we are on a swing; as a child swings higher and higher, we are gently rocking between the two motions of creation and ascension, moving from the inflow to outflow, moving from the ascending wave to the descending wave and back again to the ascending wave."

"It, again, is the ascending or returning wave that we must grab a hold of but, as of yet, there is still no surrender and we are now moving and rocking back and forth; our body shaking and rocking as the sound and light begin to stream in stronger and stronger, as we begin to realize that the VARDAN has taken over and there is no place where IT is not within our consciousness."

"We now stand in the center of the two waves, the ascending wave and the descending wave. The wave of Audible Life Current that sustains all and brings all into manifestation, and the wave that returns back to the Godhead, moving forever all beings and entities back into the very heart of this mighty Ocean of Love and Mercy, from where all life began and beyond all time, space, matter and energy."

"This is the eternal space of nothingness and everything. The Beingness and Isness of Isness. The all. The everything. The source of all existence. The birth place of Soul if Soul could have such a birth place and yet, Soul is eternal and beyond time, therefore it is more of the Isness of Isness. The I am therefore I am. I am he and IT is God!"

"As we begin to ascend, the returning wave has grabbed a hold of us, but the descending wave that sustains and is the all sustaining wave, has not let go as of yet."

"This is the moment of choice. Shall we surrender and let go and turn all our Beingness and self over to the Inner Master or shall we continue to hold on to the descending wave that sustains all and manifests all?"

"The returning wave or the descending wave. That manifests all the heavens and sustains all things or that which returns all Souls and consciousness to the universal oneness and completion of existence."

"In other words, returns Soul to the very Godhead itself and gives Soul the ecstatic experience of Self and God Realization!!!"

"And yet, with all this, Soul has still not surrendered unto the Master but is closer than IT might imagine. Soul stands on the razors-edge and between eternity and timelessness, between love and power, between creation and completion, between service and receiving the blessings of the HURAY. To be sustained and manifest, or return without effort or resistance to that from where Soul came."

"Terror may strike Soul and it may tremble in its boots, fearful that it may lose itself within the all returning wave that mercilessly calls out for total and complete surrender to IT. To that, that Is the Allness, the Beingness and Isness of God or HURAY of ITSELF."

"Soul will feel fear and terror, if such a thing is possible and may hesitate to continue on this path back via the light and sound."

"The rocking motion may continue with the sustaining, issuing wave moving out into this world and soul may fail to surrender to the returning wave that the Master calls upon Soul to follow, back with him to the heart of the HURAY."

"This is a magical moment and one that most Souls will fail to fulfill out of fear and ego. It is this time that Soul stands on the razor's edge of eternity. If Soul can let go of all expectation and desire, and follow the Master and this returning wave, then the rocking ceases and Soul makes an upward ascent into those worlds of blinding white light and dazzling Sound. The knowingness and beingness are beyond compare and at this moment for perhaps for the first time, Soul has surrendered to the Master and to the HURAY."

"This is not pseudo surrender but true surrender and few reach this point. There is no longer any conflict between Soul and the lower worlds, for all has been left behind as a lover abandons all qualms for his beloved."

"All feelings and doubts leave and there is an immense peace and tranquility and knowingness that occupies this moment, when Soul begins to ascend on the Audible Life Stream and merges into IT, finding IT and the Audible Life Stream are cut of the same fabric. In fact, Soul discovers through direct experience that IT is cut of the same cloth as the Master and of God, or the HURAY ITSELF and there is no longer any mind conflict, that existed when the two forces where opposed."

"This apparent opposition was an illusion and the true unification of the HURAY, VARDAN and Master is experienced as Soul cries out "I and the Father are one!!" "I am that I am!!!" All doubt and turmoil leave and the apparent contradictions and illusions of the lower worlds leave, as the Audible Life Stream takes Soul into the worlds beyond all thought and opposites."

"There is no longer a conflict and Soul has, in effect, begun its surrender to ITSELF through the total letting go of the little self, and turning over its essence to the Master with love and trust."

"This love and trust is beyond human understanding, and it has taken Soul vast stretches of time through many illusions to reach this point, where it of itself, is willing to give up itself to the HURAY, VARDAN and Master."

"When this happens, Soul is shocked to find that IT is far greater and has not lost its individuality at all, but has come to an entirely new evolutionary stage. One of total awareness, total freedom, total love and total compassion and of course, total power."

"Not the kind of power that demands anything from God, but the power of God ITSELF as ITS conscious vehicle and divine channel."

"This is a topic that can hardly be spoken of and I say onto you that although there is much to say, words cannot fully describe what I am speaking of, for it only can be experienced during the spiritual exercises of VARDANKAR. This is why we must learn to die daily and become born anew. The depth of what I am speaking of transcends thought and no one will understand it, until they are within the throes of the Great Audible Life Stream, and have let go and surrendered their Soul or true God self onto that stream, that returns back into the heart of God or HURAY. This is the way. The method used by all true spiritual travelers and those of the VARDAN Masters, who lead man beyond the lower worlds into the Atma Lok, Alakh Lok, Alaya Lok, Hukikat Lok, Agam Lok, Anami Lok and beyond."

"Come now and listen to the divine words of Yaubl Sacabi who acts as the guardian of the Gare Hira Golden Wisdom Temple and is in charge of this world and has many spiritual duties involving the return of Souls to the Great HURAY in their respective lifetimes."

"I bring you now, Yaubl Sacabi." Rebazar pointed opening his hands widely.

Out of the darkness appeared Yaubl. His aura was a shining beacon of white golden light and his smile and the kindness of his eyes was extraordinary. Gazing into them was like gazing into windows to the Ocean of Love and Mercy of ITSELF.

It was strange that I had not noticed this nearly as much, until now, just how bright this being was.

Then he began to speak.

YS: "Listen dear Souls, for I come in peace to bear the sacred message of the HURAY or God onto this dark and humble world. I am but a humble channel for IT, the Audible Life Stream or voice of the HURAY, the consciousness and Love, Wisdom, Power and Freedom that transcends all human understanding."

"Surrender to that which is eternal and heed not illusion. Do not fear the mundane, the rocks of karma that solidify in the mind like concrete or limestone that hardens like petrified fossils, or the bones of some prehistoric animal incased in rock that has become rock and hardened into solid matter or mind stuff too dense to be of use."

"The sweet call of the Bani or Sound Current, the Audible Life Stream is calling but is man listening? Can man surrender to it or will he resist ITS call to him to return back to Soul's divine beginnings."

"The HURAY waits patiently, the Master waits for Soul to come to the realization that all there is in life is the HURAY, VARDAN and the divine consciousness, as found in the Audible Life Stream or divine light and sound current, that flows from the Ocean of Love and Mercy or the Godhead."

"We can ignore this Audible Life Stream. We can try and be selective in how to follow it or at what level we wish to go with it and surrender to it. But when we are selective or pick and choose within our own limited comfort zone of the ego or little self, we are like the child who cannot leave his parent and must hide in safety in the mundane worlds of illusion."

"We are fearful and when we are fearful, we are not free. Our heart is heavy and we are without God. We become isolated and lonely and cry out not understanding that it is us, who has isolated our self from God and not God that has isolated us from IT."

"God awaits us with all the patience imaginable. It sends its only representative, the Margatma, the Living VARDAN Master to greet Soul and show it the way back home unto IT."

"IT offers Soul truth, knowing that most will reject truth and try and pick and choose their method of returning to IT."

"When one refuses to acknowledge the true way and places subtle demands upon God or HURAY and demands God bring him home in a particular way, shape or form, then one is spitting in the face of God."

"God cannot be reasoned with, bargained with, or convinced of anything for God is not a thing, idea, ideal, or emotion. God is not even a state of consciousness. No, we do not bargain with God and demand that God do things our way. We must surrender to that which is pure and unchanging and give up and surrender our very Soul to the Audible Life Stream and the Inner Master. Then we find happiness, contentment and truth for now we are real and unchanging; as before, we based our lives on the temporal and mundane."

"We cannot demand that God do things our way; we must

do things as God has always wanted Soul, to follow ITS ways and ITS one unchanging law: the law of Love."

"The law of Universal Love is only found in the Audible Life Stream and in this, only in the returning wave of this stream that returns Soul back to it. All else is of a lower nature."

"Even the great sustaining wave of all creation pales in comparison to that returning wave that carries Soul back to the great Ocean of Love and Mercy, where the HURAY has its humble abode."

"Only there, does Soul find truth and the unchanging eternal reality of the HURAY."

"Then Soul may ride the all sustaining wave back down into the lower worlds while simultaneously maintaining contact with the eternal HURAY, the unchanging eternal reality of the great fountain of life, the VARDAN the Audible Life Stream."

"It is through surrender to this returning wave that Soul finds eternal life and the endless wellspring of all Love, Wisdom, Power and Freedom. It is the returning wave that brings Soul to see the true face of God and cry out "I am He! I am that I am! I and the Father are one!"

"It is this great returning wave of the Audible Life Stream, the VARDAN or light and sound of HURAY that leads to truth; for what is truth but the unchanging HURAY and ITS consciousness, ITS breath and Soul's individual eternal experience of IT."

"All Souls will have their own experience of the HURAY."

"No Soul has ever found all of IT for IT is not a thing, nor is IT limited in any way, shape or form nor can IT be defined. It contains both an inside and an outside. The inside is that which nothing can be said about and contains no qualities at all. Nothing can be said about this part of the HURAY."

"The outside of the HURAY or Saguna is a different story and is the expression of all qualities and the totality of consciousness on all visible and invisible planes, from the highest to the lowest. It is the voice of the HURAY and has unlimited qualities and aspects and contains the all within the All. It is the seed within the seed and nothing can be said, except it contains such qualities as, Love, Wisdom, Power and Freedom; and is the outward expression of the Allness, Beingness and Seeingness of God: the Omnipresence, Omniscience and Omnipotence. Soul, too, has this inside and outside, but cannot find this truth without first surrendering completely to the returning wave mentioned before."

"This is done through the Margatma, the Inner Master who is the VARDAN of ITSELF and the personification or personalization of the HURAY here on Earth. This is necessary for man to make the vast jump from the lower states to the higher states, using the VARDAN initiations, the Audible Life Stream, the Master and the HURAY. Without this combination, Soul is generally lost in a sea of confusion and illusion. Those who falsely think they can beat this system are sadly mistaken and will find eventually that the way of pain and incarnations is a long hard road and that the wise Soul follows the path of VARDANKAR, which is the most direct path back to God via the Ancient Science of Out-of-Body Tuza Travel, via the Sound Current."

"Only those true VARDAN Masters can teach this science from the higher worlds and all others only teach man how to reach the universal mind power on the mental plane or the Brahm or Kal in the astral and causal worlds."

"Man will spit upon the face of the Living VARDAN Master but he does not generally complain, for he understands the deep suffering that man will endure for his defiance in following the path of the light and sound or VARDAN, back to God."

"There now, you have been given the true meaning of the word surrender."

"Here is a simple method you can follow. You may rock back and forth and let go of all fear and attachment and allow the Sound Current of the returning wave to grab a hold of you and go with it and the Inner Master, to where he will lead you."

"You may place the image of the Inner Master upon the screen of your mind and let it purify you. Place it in the Tisra Til or third eye, located between the eye brows about an inch inside the skull. Gaze into this dark region and see the shining inner face of the Living VARDAN Master or another spiritual traveler there, purifying your every thought, deed and emotion."

"You may declare yourself a vehicle for the VARDAN, HURAY and Master and declare that every word, action and deed is done in the name of the Inner Master, the VARDAN and the HURAY."

"You may let go of all preconceived notions, ideas, opinions and fears you may have. Letting go of all qualms and disharmony and be harmonious in the thought that all is well within this returning wave of the Audible Life Stream, the VARDAN and that the Inner Master, the Margatma, the Living VARDAN Master is with you at all times and as close as your heart beat."

"Surrender now! Do not fear. Now you know it is not just the little self that must be surrendered but Soul, your true Self. You must follow the returning wave back to God via the

Margatma, the Living VARDAN Master or one of his appointees, the true spiritual travelers such as myself, Rebazar Tarzs, Fubbi Quantz or many others such as Rami Nuri or Kata Daki."

"There is nothing you cannot accomplish, if you will but become a humble channel for God and let go of the little self completely. Then you shall lose all fear of life and death and die daily during your contemplations without fear of death, nor life."

"Then you will become alive with the VARDAN and be spiritually free and have access to all Love, Wisdom, Freedom and Power, not to control your fellow man but to be a great and humble channel for this light and sound, which now flows through you and is you."

"You are the VARDAN and the VARDAN is you!"

"That is all I have to say for now."

"Go in peace and fear not the Kal power or its agents, but love the VARDAN and HURAY with all your heart, body, mind and Soul!!"

And with that Yaubl Sacabi disappeared, leaving me to ponder his mighty and wise words.

23

MAN'S MISUNDERSTANDING OF DIVINE IMAGINATION

Rebazar appeared serious and gazed out into what appeared to be the universes of God, as a man might gaze off into the distance from a top some high mountain on a clear summer's day and view all below with serenity and detachment. But this time, there was an air of mystery as if this great Tibetan lama and VARDAN Master was pondering some hidden riddle of timeless importance.

RT: "Man misunderstands the nature of divine imagination and this, frankly is his downfall and end."

"In the beginning, the mighty HURAY existed at the top of all worlds and dreamed. There was really nothing that could be said about this. As I have spoken of beforehand, the HURAY has two sides: the inside or what is known as the Nirguna and the outside which is known as the Saguna."

"Now the inside has no qualities but the outside brings forth consciousness that, although man may barely speak of it, is actually the expression or should I say the HURAY's expression."

"Words are not adequate nor even work in any of this and

yet, I will try for your benefit to express the inexpressible."

"Anyway, it is true in a rather poetic way that the HURAY dreams ... or is capable of dreaming. Of course, IT is all things and IT is No-thing. There are qualities and yet, there are no qualities. How does one understand the un-understandable?"

"Yes, he cannot do this ... except he may understand his very nature and the nature of the HURAY through observation, but mostly through the conscious participation of life."

"We may observe all we want but we must also participate. Thus, Out-of-Body Tuza or Soul Travel is the way. In this, we participate in life. Not just the mundane physical life of the ordinary man but the cosmic life of the Allness, the Beingness of Total Awareness, Total Consciousness and Total Responsibility."

"Man fears this, but that is because he is ignorant and must be taught by the Spiritual Travelers the truth, so that he may become a God-man like myself and find spiritual freedom and truth."

"The ignorant will claim that truth cannot be found or that truth is found in dogma and religion; in books and the personality or certain persona of a being such as Jesus or Mohammed or Krishna."

"The divine dreamer is the HURAY, but Soul as a particle of HURAY has within it the ability to dream as the HURAY dreams."

"This is a great gift from the HURAY. One of many great gifts that man possesses but does not know he possesses or has little awareness of this."

"At first Soul begins to squander this gift of divine dreaming or divine imagination. He uses it to defeat his enemies, to acquire the things of this world."

"This only creates karma, for man is more interested in power and control than in God and service to God as a conscious co-creator or co-worker."

"Man squanders his divine dreaming abilities or perhaps worse, forgets that they even exist at all!"

"There have been numerous books and teachings about this but frankly, they are kindergarten teachings that only teach the petty manifestation of money, human love and the Kal attributes."

"Still, it does make my point, that the power of dreaming or divine imagination is all powerful."

"How can this be? Because simply, it is a part of spirit or the VARDAN. Most men squander this and use it in the lower states of consciousness and for this, they must suffer reincarnation and karma, which they dream up and create for themselves and others. In a vain attempt, they confuse eternity with longevity! The finite with the infinite and their dreams are of a materialistic nature, focusing on the things of this world such as human love, compassion, wealth, health, power, emotional freedom, good will towards mankind, the helping of bodies or embodiments, the acquisition of material wisdom and intellectual understandings about the lower nature of the psychic forces that sustain the lower worlds and so forth. What they fail to understand is that, if they would only surrender their true Self Soul to the Living VARDAN Master, they could have Truth. Not this false truth or shadow of truth, but the real truth, the source of all. The truth found beyond the lower worlds in the Anami Lok and beyond this, into the very heart of the

HURAY where truth and beingness can be experienced."

"The divine dreamer sells himself short by listening to the whisperings of the Kal Niranjan or king of the negative power."

"He listens to the scientists, the religionists, the metaphysicians, his local priest, bishop, and the various self-help authors and fake gurus who permeate this world. It is said that a little bit of knowledge is dangerous? Yes, it certainly can hinder Soul on its path back to the HURAY for when one dreams of lesser things, they will squander their time in the lower worlds in a state of semi consciousness and this can go on for millions of lifetimes or until a Spiritual Traveler makes contact with the individual and he is able to accept the challenge of finding truth through dying daily during his spiritual exercises and surrender to the Inner Master."

"Then, and only then, will he have a chance at finding truth or Self and God realization within this lifetime or the next."

"Returning to the subject of divine imagination and man's misunderstanding of it, man does not really understand much of anything. He drifts in and out of illusion upon illusion and, quite frankly, until he desires truth more than lies, he will continue in this vein in beseeching God for his material, emotional and mental needs ad infinitum."

"Man will misuse his divine imagination or ability to dream and try and acquire all manner of things but, mostly, man is asleep and dreams not of what he wants, but is in a state of sleep and is at the effect of his own creations and past and present thoughts."

"He is in a sort of dream-like state but has little control over it since he refuses to seek truth and only the emotional or astral influences seem to delight his senses. He seeks comfort in the touch of a woman or in the eating of rich foods. In the buying of expensive items found in various markets and in the exercise of power over his fellow man, thinly disguised as service to God, his country or the corporation that he happens to work for."

"Man is confused. He does not know what exactly he is or what he wants. He does not understand the great power that has been entrusted to him by the HURAY. This is, of course, the divine imagination that lay dormant or partly dormant within him."

"Man maligns imagination, even fearing it. He maligns dreams and what he calls pie in the sky attitudes."

"Be practical he shouts, seek the comforts of this world, seek approval and admiration, power and wealth, health and good will from other men who will befriend and protect you from harm's way. Seek the favor of the space god and the space god will provide all your material, emotional and mental needs and even a final place to stay in heaven that will make a Hawaiian paradise pale by comparison."

"This is the worst sort of salesmanship. It is like the used car salesman, who is selling a rusted out piece of junk as a Cadillac and fine automobile. If anyone wants to spend the next 10 thousand years in the mid Astral Plane wasting precious time, they certainly can aim for such a foolish goal. But it is only temporary and most likely, they will end up back on Earth for more incarnations."

"One can waste their good karma on this sort of false dream of happiness and bliss, or they can use their good karma to earn them a meeting with the Living VARDAN Master and to be accepted as a chela on the path of Out-of-Body Tuza Travel, where they can have the opportunity to reach their second initiation and never have to incarnate on Earth again as a sleeping Soul."

"They can work out all their Earthly karma, and begin to dwell in those worlds that saints and mystics have spoken of but that few men know of, let alone, consciously dwell in."

"These worlds of golden white light and sound are truly beyond description."

"To use one's divine imagination to meet with the Master and learn to consciously dwell in the higher worlds of God is the proper use of imagination."

"In a Kali Yuga, of which we are in now, also known as the Iron Age or age of negativity, man reverses everything."

"The virtuous becomes evil and the evil becomes virtuous."

"Man sees the good as bad and the bad as good. Fools are seen as kings and kings are seen as fools."

"Now man laughs at divine imagination and even suggests the use of psychiatric drugs, electro shock therapy and psychological counseling for those who dare to use it more than society deems acceptable."

"The Kal does not want Soul to use divine imagination properly."

"The proper use of divine imagination is to become one with the Divine Dreamer. To recognize our innate ability, to wish and enter into any state of consciousness, to enter into any world we desire. To even create those worlds that we desire out of the fabric of God itself, the Divine VARDAN that sustains all life and is undifferentiated Love, Wisdom, Power, Freedom and beyond this."

"All things come to those who wait. But they must have divine imagination and be properly schooled in its use."

"Divine imagination or the imaginative faculty within Soul itself, our eternal unchanging self is, in effect, a part of the enormous unfathomable power of the HURAY stepped down into a single Soul who can use it or abuse it at will."

"Should a Soul abuse this power, it will suffer and get less and less of it to abuse."

"Should a Soul follow the true Spiritual Travelers, the VARDAN Masters, they will use this power wisely; which is to become this power, and use it for the good of the whole and in accord with the divine plan of the HURAY, working naturally with the great law of universal love or good will."

"Man does not want this, because he desires to control things through his little ego self and his meager mind!"

"Ha!!!!" Rebazar barked out loud, as if to make a point."

R.T. "If man only knew the pain this inflicts upon him. For when he desires to control the universal power of divine imagination from the egocentric consciousness of the Kal, he creates a cascading effect of karma and reincarnation the likes of which, if he understood, he would immediately cease and realize he has been his own worst enemy in life!"

"There is a sort of war going on between the children of light and the children of darkness. This is not between good and evil, so much, as the children of the Kal vs. the children of the VARDAN."

"One group desires that Soul suffer in darkness and ignorance in the lower worlds and the other, the true VARDANists, desires that Soul be free and be given the opportunity to dwell inwardly in the Higher Worlds beyond matter, energy, time, space and the universal mind power."

"These two groups are in dire opposition to one another, the Kal group desiring to destroy the VARDAN group at all cost."

"This war manifests itself in the malalignment of divine imagination."

"Imagination is considered bad in this world by most everyone."

"The trite sayings are almost endless. "It's not real" "Stop daydreaming and live your life" "Pay attention!" And so on and so forth. Man's imagination is deemed by so called modern science, which is really pseudo-science, to be a series of chemical and electrical brain and neurological activities that have nothing to do with reality outside our physical bodies!"

"The psychiatric community has termed such things as paranoid, delusional, and the hearing of voices is considered very serious."

"There are, of course, many who go out of balance and need help, and I am not saying that anyone who comes unglued is a spiritual giant or that there is no such thing as mental and emotional illness. What I am saying is that man is attacking imagination and, in this, he is attacking God! Or, more accurately, that aspect of God that allows man to return to it!

"Now, of course, man must have the sound current to return. Imagination by itself, is useless without the Audible Life Stream running through it to enliven and empower and draw it upwards into the higher worlds, with the guidance of the true way shower, the Living VARDAN Master."

"But imagination and the abilities of the Divine Dreamer are a part of Soul and of the HURAY and are sacred."

"To put them down in any way is to declare war on God ITSELF!"

"This is the God power that man must use, along with the VARDAN initiations, total reliance on the Inner Master and the spiritual exercises of VARDANKAR."

"As stated before, the initiations and the Audible Life Stream of the light and sound of the HURAY, must be linked through the Living VARDAN Master and in this we have, for perhaps the first time, the opportunity for spiritual liberation within this lifetime and not have to spin around and around on the 'wheel of 84' for millions upon millions of lifetimes."

"If one is not willing to go back to God now or in this lifetime, then what guarantee does he have that he will do this upon the death of his physical body? None I say. Absolutely none."

"If one does not recognize the opportunity now or wants to postpone this opportunity to some future date and place, then this future date may be a very long time indeed. In fact, there are many who have taken up the path of VARDANKAR which was, of course, known throughout history under various different names and faces. And then they quit the path and go off. Some of these people have had to wait for thousands of years before another opportunity comes around for them."

"Those who shun the path, claiming they just want to live their life from a material, psychic, emotional and mental state of awareness are, of course, free to do this. But if they understood what they were doing, they would know they were missing a great opportunity and may have to wait thousands of even millions of years before it comes again. This is what happens to those who postpone their desire to return to God. They get their wish fulfilled. They truly postpone the event into some unforeseen future date and time."

"Trouble is that the divine dream happens now. Not in the future. So they become trapped on the time track of the Kal worlds where the Kal plays them for a fool. Then they, generally, end up meeting some false guru who teaches them to focus on one of their lower chakras and play around with the lower forces of nature. This only wastes more time but, of course, time is all they have and plenty of it. Since Soul exists within eternity, Soul waits patiently for the Inner Master to do something but if they refuse, they must wait until the time comes when they appreciate truth and love truth and God more than their own petty defilements and psychic urges for the things of the lower worlds."

"Divine imagination is the answer."

"Dare we dream? Dare we dream? Dare we dream?"

Rebazar paused as if wanting me to answer, but then he answered for me.

RT: "Yes!! I say only the fool fails to participate in the divine dream ... to use his divine imagination to find spiritual freedom and follow the Master into the splendid worlds of God!!"

"Yes Dream. Do not listen to those who preach the ways of the Kal and tell you that imagination and dreaming is not real. That it is false."

"Now having said all of this, I have to say something that may confuse some of you. That is, as you know in the lower worlds, all things exist in direct opposition to their polar opposites. In other words, these are the dual worlds where, without love, we cannot have hate and vice versa. Without darkness there can be no light, etc."

"So what does this have to do with what I am speaking of today?"

"Simply this: Man must know that there are many illusions. He will view these through his divine imagination and he must not throw the baby out with the bath water."

"He must use the various methods as taught by the VARDAN Masters in order to reach God. Without these secret methods he would, quite frankly, be without hope or have little hope of reaching Self and God Realization. This is because of these great opposites and this extreme Maya or illusion that exists down in these lower worlds of M.E.S.T. (matter, energy, space, and time)"

"Man can use the matrix or image of the Living VARDAN Master or another VARDAN Master, such as myself, and place that image within the screen of the mind or the Tisra Til, located between the eye brows about an inch inside the skull."

"Man simply sees the shining face of the Master and imagines that all streams of consciousness, coming to the individual and coming away from the individual, are moving through the Master's presence or consciousness. This allows the Inner Master to purify all thoughts and mental and emotional impressions, coming into and out of the individual Soul's consciousness."

"One must declare themselves a conscious vehicle for the

VARDAN, the Margatma and the HURAY and do all things in the name of the VARDAN, Margatma and HURAY."

"One must practice total sincerity and desire God more than anything else."

"One must practice selflessness and relax in a child-like expectancy; that God and the Master is taking care of them and that everything that happens to them is for their spiritual benefit."

"This is, of course, true. Even when a chela of the Master suffers, this is a part of Soul's spiritual education and learning experience."

"But, now, the true VARDANist is focused on truth and finding Self and God Realization, instead of all the Kal distractions he used to be sucked into, such as ego, money, power, control and material success."

"He may still have a nice car, a loving wife, etc., but he has now become detached to the things of this world and should he lose them, it will not upset him too greatly because his priorities are now on God or HURAY and no longer on the Kal values and illusions. He has switched from the dreams and nightmares of the Kal, king of the lower worlds, to the Divine Dream of God Realization and conscious co-workership with the HURAY."

"This is a quantum shift and any quantum shift is bound to cause problems at first."

"All manner of obstacles will come and go and the individual may think that all heaven and Earth will swallow him up."

"But this again is just another illusion by the Kal or negative to try and prevent man from reaching true God Realization and finding truth."

"Most men do not believe one can find truth. They believe in the space god and finding favor with the space god who manages their lives in the form of power, wealth, health, and the comforts of the physical world and the astral afterlife, where angels fly around on wings of silk and babies play harps or some similar lower world heavenly vision that, quite frankly, would make me quite bored in a matter of hours!"

"There are such places on the Astral Plane where angels fly around and play harps and there are large banquet tables with golden cups and so forth. These were actually created by Souls who imagined them into existence!!"

"But these are not even remotely close to the great worlds or far country, past the Mental and Etheric Plane."

"Allen, I had spoken of surrendering to the great VARDAN sound current and how one may rock back and forth like a sailor on the sea of life. But that when one chooses the returning wave, they are carried into the very heart of God and into a state of total surrender to the Inner Master and VARDAN."

"Eventually, this leads to God Realization and becoming a member of the order of the Boucharan, that brotherhood of VARDAN Masters who are responsible for aiding Souls in returning back to the HURAY."

"Now I say this. This divine Imagination is the great two-edged sword of life itself."

"Use it wisely and it shall bring you all things that are eternal, namely Self Realization, God Realization and VARDAN

Mastership."

"Use it foolishly and we have entrapment within the lower worlds of time and space. We have disillusionment, illusion and maya. We have confusion and so the saying goes, 'that the road to God is strewn with the corpses of those who have failed!'"

"So I tell you that you must not fear anything! Nothing must faze you! Only the bold, adventurous, resourceful and cunning will find God, so you might as well take these words to heart and know that without divine imagination, you are dead in the water."

"It must be used no matter what. And if you fail to use it consciously, it will be used unconsciously."

"Every time you project into the future or even the present, you are generally using this faculty."

"Man's mind spins, but this is because he has not learned to go beyond the mind and engage in Tuza Travel above the lower worlds."

"Man must relax and surrender to the spiritual traveler. Then he must learn to be patient and sincere in his desire for truth and for God. Then he must have the eyes to see and the ears to hear truth."

"He must be cunning and resourceful, bold and adventurous. Leave all fear by the wayside and develop that child-like state of freedom and imagination without fear or concern for his own petty little self."

"Then, when he surrenders to the Inner Master, all things will be given unto him as he gives all things to the Master."

"That is all for this morning."

"Go and rest now."

"Know I love you beyond measure and only desire that you return, that man returns to God and reaches a greater more expansive measure of consciousness. This can be achieved through VARDANKAR the ancient science of Tuza or Soul Travel."

24

DEATH AND THE NECESSITY OF DYING DAILY IN ORDER TO FIND GOD

I was strangely aware that this series of dialogues was about to end and that this might be the last and final one.

There was a calm tiredness inside of me, an unsettling feeling that something was missing; that I had somehow missed something important.

Then, Rebazar appeared before me in a rather somber mood.

RT: "You seem disappointed? Did not these dialogues enlighten and entertain ye?"

AF: "That was not the point, was it?"

RT: "Well, perhaps not the entertainment part, but enlighten? Perhaps not that either. If then neither, then what possible use are they to the world?"

AF: "Perhaps they serve as an inspiration?"

RT: "Well"...Rebazar paused as if thinking. "Most...you know this for yourself ... most will either like or dislike them but in the end, do nothing. This is the lazy nature of mankind. He wants to be entertained and amused and given a big show, but then he is off for the next round of amusements. He does not really understand any of the secret works of VARDANKAR but thinks that he does."

"The whole of the outer works is but an inner gateway into the secret teachings of the Ancient Masters and those enlightened beings who call themselves the VARDAN adepts."

"They may go by many names but you and I know who they are, but most do not. Most fail because they never really wanted to have God or travel to God. They only want to imagine this as a child might imagine being a world famous baseball player. But when push comes to shove, they do not want to put in any real effort to finding truth, nor do they want to give anything up. And this, my friend, is to a large degree the problem."

"Most men are either too lazy or too scared to find truth."

"They would rather watch some sports on TV or read a book, then do the work necessary to find God Realization."

"And, perhaps, this is the way it should be. For if they found God, they would not know what to do next! One must be ready for the experience and thus, the Master prepares his chelas so that they may find truth and express it in like, as conscious vehicles for the Master and the HURAY."

"There is nothing else in life that gives more pleasure than to surrender or the act of self-surrender."

"Man must learn to die daily. This he fears and yet, quite ironically, until man learns to die daily and enter into the supreme consciousness of the higher worlds, he is dead. He is dead until he learns to die daily. What precisely is he dying to?

"It is to the human condition the little self."

"When man returns to this body, he resumes his partaking in the lower bodies as tools in his service to God. They are necessary for his universal work; for as long as he lives in these lower worlds, he must have these bodies."

"However, they have stopped in out-creating him and now, he is truly alive for he has learned to venture into those worlds beyond matter, energy, space and time, where the universal sound current is so overwhelming that man becomes the VARDAN of ITSELF, while maintaining his individuality. He becomes born anew and is a new creature, not of this Earth world but of another origin. That of the universal worlds of light and sound, the God worlds above duality and mind!"

"Man must learn to die daily in order to be truly alive; for in these higher worlds man is alive! More alive than anyone of a mortal nature could possibly understand ... unless, of course, they themselves are Spiritual Travelers such as yourself."

"Even you have only a rough idea of the totality and oneness, the power and love that are yours, if you will but completely and utterly surrender yourself to the Beingness and Isness of the HURAY."

"Even as I speak, there are certain readers that are confused as to why I am saying this to you even though you are the Master?"

"How could this be? Well perhaps in the inner you know all things but on the outer, you have your limitations as you are well aware of. This is true of myself as well, but I have had over 550 years to perfect my lower bodies and you have had scarcely a few months as the Living VARDAN Master of our times.

What was it, in October of last year that you took the rod of power and became the Master?"

"Man desires to find some personality to worship but this is, frankly, his downfall and yours as well, if you fall for such foolishness."

"Returning to the subject at hand, when man learns to die daily he leaves his body during his spiritual exercises or during the dream state and consciously partakes of those states of consciousness beyond the body and lower self."

"He then returns to this body as I said before, born anew."

"His inner awareness and scope of consciousness has totally changed, although he may not be able to prove this to his fellow man, nor even be sure it is true ... it is nonetheless true."

"This is the secret, or at least one of the great secrets and why the Master says over and over again, that his chelas must practice the spiritual exercises daily if they desire results."

"It is this dying daily that produces miracles but not of a materialistic nature, but of a spiritual nature."

"Most men are not interested in consciousness; only in their stomachs, fortune, health and sex life. They care not about consciousness; and are of a brutish disposition, or of an intellectually mental disposition or emotional bent."

"They are of this world, and do not desire to be anywhere else but here in these lower worlds and, quite frankly, the Maser does not care; for these are the unready Souls who must wait until they are ready and the Master once again gives them an opportunity to find the high path once again."

"The Master will give his chelas the methods or modus operandi to not only leave their body, but reach a position of spiritual freedom within this lifetime if at all possible. If the person is older and does not have enough time on this Earth, they may have to reach spiritual liberation in the next life, but as long as they remain loyal to the Master and to VARDANKAR, they will find spiritual liberation within this lifetime or the next."

"This is, of course, provided they practice the spiritual exercises and follow the teachings to the best of their spiritual abilities."

"The act of dying daily is one of realizing the power of attention and understanding the nature of dual awareness."

"We may become aware of many bodies at the same time. We may be aware of the breathing of our physical body, the feelings of our emotional body and the thoughts of our mental apparatus all at the same time. We may have ridiculous thoughts at times and wonder if the Kal will stop us from meeting with the Master."

"But the chela must understand that he is already with the Master at all times, that there is no need to find the Master for he is already there. However, he must place his attention upon that which already is."

"This is done through beingness and beingness is accomplished, generally, through imagination and attention. But there is however a better way, that of placing one's attention upon the Inner Sound Current of VARDAN. That sound that travels in the returning wave and completely surrendering to the Master and VARDAN … never looking back."

"When one rides the divine sound current, they are

spiritually free as long as they keep their attention squarely upon the Master and God."

"If their attention is split, they can simply watch their thoughts and feelings float by like gently floating barges on a river and not get excited, but relax in a child-like expectation that God and the Master are taking care of everything."

"When one chants their secret word given to them during their 2nd initiation or higher or in the case of the acolyte, chants one of the holy names or sounds of the God worlds, they may let the sound current carry them away in consciousness without fear that anything bad will happen to their physical body."

"The Master or one of the other VARDAN Masters will watch the body and see to it that no harm comes to it."

"This dying daily is centered in the fact that the true VARDAN initiate always dwells in the Higher Worlds!"

"Time and space being an illusion, all must find truth in the here and now of the moment. This truth is not of a mental, physical nor emotional nature, but eternal, unchanging and is beyond thought. It is pure consciousness and beingness and can only be experienced. When one meets with the various VARDAN Masters in the various Golden Wisdom Temples of VARDAN, they are prepared for this truth that will enter into their consciousness and bring them to Self and God Realization or Total Awareness."

"Man can see the face of God. This is his birthright, for man and God are cut of the same cloth. However, the ego self or lower self cannot come on this journey. The lower self is far too dense to enter into the Higher Worlds... therefore, man must die daily leaving his body in order to experience these higher states."

"This is the whole point in a nut shell and, frankly, this is why man will never find truth in books, lectures or in any earthly activities."

"The outer teachings of VARDANKAR are not to be worshipped, for they are little more than a gateway to truth."

"They are the door and not the whole room."

"In God's house, there are many mansions or states of consciousness and it is man's solemn duty to discover God through the Ancient Science of Out-of-Body Tuza travel."

"This ends this book and this series of discourses."

"May the Blessings Be."

And with that, Rebazar went off into his mountain world to leave me pondering his words.

THE END.

ABOUT THE AUTHOR

Allen Feldman is an accomplished Soul Traveler with over thirty three years of Out-of-Body experiences ranging from traveling throughout the Physical, Astral, Casual, Mental, Etheric and the various Pure Positive God Worlds including the Anami Lok and beyond. Allen is also Self and God Realized and has established himself deep within the Heart of God (HURAY) while maintaining a physical body in order to serve here on Earth and the other various lower planes of Matter, Energy, Time and Space. He is also currently The Margatma, the Living VARDAN Master and head of VARDANKAR, the Ancient Science of Out-Of-Body Tuza (Soul) Travel.

Allen works with his students on the outer through the writing of books, study discourses and other outer works as well as on the Inner Planes or worlds during the dream state and waking life. He writes and speaks about the subjects of Out-of-Body Travel, Self-Realization, Spiritual Experiences, God-Realization and various other related topics including Reincarnation, Karma, Spiritual Exercises, and the true purpose of why we are here in this world.

Allen works with the Ancient VARDAN Masters who have been kind enough to share with him and his readers their deep esoteric wisdom and experiences of the highest order. The secret knowledge of how to return back to the source of all of life, the HURAY or God, far above the lower psychic worlds.

THE GOD HEAVENS/WORLDS OF VARDANKAR

NAME OF PLANE	WORD	CLASSICAL NAME	SOUND
ABOVE 12 PLANES . . . HURAY REALIZATION . . .			
12. HURAY	UNSPOKEN WORD	HURAY-LIVING REALITY	MUSIC OF GOD
11. HURAY WORLD	UNSPOKEN WORD	HURAY LOK	MUSIC OF UNIVERSE
10. ANAMI LOK	HU	ANAMI LOK	SOUND OF A WHIRLPOOL
9. AGAM LOK	HUK	AGAM LOK	MUSIC OF THE WOODWINDS
8. HUKIKAT LOK	ALUK	HUKIKAT LOK	THOUSAND VIOLINS
7. ALAYA LOK	HUM	ALAYA LOK	DEEP HUMMING
6. ALAKH LOK	SHANTI	ALAKH LOK	HEAVY WIND
5. SOUL	HURAY	SAT NAM	SINGLE NOTE OF A FLUTE
▬▬▬▬▬▬▬▬▬▬▬▬▬▬▬▬ DIVIDING LINE BETWEEN PSYCHIC ▬▬			
ETHERIC TOP OF MENTAL	BAJU	SAGUNA-SAGUNA-BRAHM INTUITION	BUZZING OF BEES
4. MENTAL	AUM	BRAHMANDA BRAHM MIND	RUNNING WATER
3. CAUSAL	MANA	MAHA-KAL-PAR-BRAHM MEMORY	TINKLE OF BELLS
2. ASTRAL	KALA	SAT KANWAL-ANDA EMOTION	ROAR OF THE SEA
1. PHYSICAL	ALAYI	ELAM. . . SENSES	THUNDER

RULER	DESCRIPTION
HURAY	OCEAN OF LOVE AND MERCY - Indescribable light and sound. Formless. All knowing, all powerfull, all present. Above the HURAY are many planes not yet realized . . .
HURAY	Out of this heaven flows the sound current of God. Beyond description. Incredible white light. Incredibly vast realm goes on forever. Formless.
ANAMI PURUSHA	NAMELESS PLANE - Beyond human language - Indescribable soft white light with whirlpool sounds-Composed of pure spirit. The begining of God Realization.
AGAM PURUSHA	INACCESSIBLE PLANE - Few enter into this world. No words can desccibe it. - Spiritual power and creativity. Here Soul learns it is the creator of its own worlds.
HUKIKAT PURUSHA	HIGHEST STATE Soul generally reaches - Soul stays here for eons. . .
ALAYA PURUSHA	ENDLESS WORLD - SACH KHAND - Eternity seems to begin and end here - unknown world. . . Endless vast light that seems to go on forever.
ALAKH PURUSHA	INVISIBLE PLANE - A vast world of yellow white light - Soul finds peace and happiness, does not want to leave - The ruler appears as a vast colossal sun like light- Supreme creative energy.
SAT NAM	DIVIDING PLANE - First realm of the HURAY - First of the Pure Positive Worlds - pure spirit, pure being, pure seeing without mind. Freedom and individuality - Self-Realization.

■ ■■ ■ AND SPIRITUAL WORLDS ■

RULER	DESCRIPTION
SOHANG	UNCONSCIOUS - Source of the primitive. - Some are fooled into thinking they have reached God Realization and there is nothing beyond this plane. Top of Mental Plane.
OMKAR	JEHOVAH - Source of philosophy, ethics, moral teachings and aesthetics. Universal Mind Power - God of Religions -Cosmic consciousness - Illusion of finding God and Heaven.
RAMKAR	KAL NIRANJAN - Rules over negative reality, effects all planes below him. - The causual is a lower source of past life records "Akashic records" - Many beleve they are in Heaven.
JOT NIRANJAN	TIRYA PAD - Source of all psychic phenomena, magic, spirits, etc. - Highest state reached by astral projection and most occult teachings - Varies from lower "dark" to higher light and joyous.
	PINDA -Plane of matter, energy, space and time - Illusion of reality - Daily "life" - Science- Soul is trapped by the five passions: anger, lust, greed, attachment and vanity.

For more information on VARDANKAR go to www.VARDANKAR.com or to find other books by Allen Feldman go to www.DirectPathPublishing.com

The Author is available to speak on radio, TV or give interviews for print and internet media. To contact the Author email Direct Path Publishing at info@DirectPathPublishing.com

DIALOGUES WITH THE MASTERS

Made in the USA
Monee, IL
02 April 2021

64622437R00154